MARRYING AGAIN

Marrying
Again

A Guide for Christians

David Hocking

Fleming H. Revell Company
Old Tappan, New Jersey

Library of Congress Cataloging in Publication Data
Hocking, David L.
  Marrying again.
    1. Remarriage—Religious aspects—Christianity.
2. Remarriage. I. Title.
BV838.H63   1983   248.8′4   82-18543
ISBN 0-8007-1338-9

TO
all of the remarried couples who have
helped me write this book.

Contents

Introduction

You may have picked up this book because:

- You are a Christian who is considering marrying again or who is actually in the process of remarriage.
- Or, you are a Christian who has remarried and you are struggling with problems which you did not expect.

What I have to say to you is from the point of view of a pastor who must counsel with men and women who find themselves in one or the other of the above groups.

My wife and I are happily married. We have never been divorced and we have no intention of ever being divorced. God had been good to us and we are most thankful for our marriage. However, many of our close friends have been divorced and are remarried, and they have shared their burdens and their heartaches with us; we have wept with them and prayed with them. We have also laughed and rejoiced with many of them for they have taught us that remarried couples can experience a wonderful marriage. From these friends we have learned much that has helped our own marriage.

As I have attempted to counsel people who are considering re-marriage I have been surprised to find that so few books and other helps are available on this subject for the Christian. That is one reason I have written this book. In these pages I will be sharing the experiences of many couples who have experienced divorce and remarriage. They have granted me permission to do so. However, to protect their privacy and guard against harming anyone, I have changed names, occupations, and certain circum-stances in the stories here included.

Many people spend their entire lifetime forming an "ideal image" of a marriage partner. They carry these expectations into a marriage and are surprised when their mates do not live up to them. This causes additional problems in the relationship that are difficult to resolve. When a marriage ends in divorce, this "ideal image" does not cease to exist; it may actually grow stronger. The expectations become even greater, often without the individual realizing it. This places a strain on a second mar-riage, especially considering the facts that those who remarry usually do so with much less preparation than when they were first married *and* the problems of remarriage are greater and de-mand more counseling than those of a first marriage.

In the first part of this book, I discuss what I consider the major problems of remarriage in the hope that by bringing them out into the open, I can help people develop more realistic ex-pectations about a second marriage. From my counseling experi-ence the problems most common in remarriage are the person's relationship to the former partner, children and stepchildren, legal matters, finances, and sexual adjustments.

I am aware of the differences of opinion among Christians re-garding divorce and remarriage and for that reason I have de-voted the first chapter to a discussion of what the Bible says on these subjects. You will see there also a treatment of the matter of *reconciliation.* It is a matter that must be resolved if the couple in question is to have confidence and peace in a new marital relationship. I always encourage those who have been divorced or who are separated to pursue every possible avenue toward reconciliation and I tell a person not to remarry until God clearly indicates that all hope of reconciliation is gone.

In this book, I am seeking to deal with realities. One of those realities, based on my own counseling experience, is that the average length of time before a remarriage takes place following divorce is approximately four months! It goes without saying that many of these people are unprepared for the problems they will encounter. So, in the first part of the book—through the shared experiences of couple after couple—I hope to shed helpful light on how to deal with these problems.

The second part of the book deals with strategies for remarriage. The person who has suffered a divorce does not want to go through that again. There are positive things to do to build a happy, enduring marriage, and those are the "strategies" which are the subject in this part of the book. I talk about forgiveness, love toward the children, and commitment.

At the end of this book you will find a Confidential Questionnaire. Two pastor friends, Paul Hoffman and Michael Moore, developed this questionnaire in a ministry to those who are marrying again and I recommend it to those who are already remarried as well. In their experience, if a person is willing to answer the fifteen questions that make up this questionnaire, he or she is probably ready to marry again.

The great need regarding the issues of divorce and remarriage is a message of healing and of hope. The wounds of the past need to be healed, and the future filled with hope. That hope must be based on a right relationship with God and biblical solutions to difficult problems. Past heartaches need to be buried beneath God's love and forgiveness.

My desire is to help. I have tried not to ignore the tough questions about divorce and remarriage. And I have sought to be flexible when biblical proof is lacking, without compromising with sin. I believe strongly in God's grace and His forgiveness and I believe that we need to hear from remarried people concerning their struggles and burdens. I have tried to listen carefully, and with their help I hope to offer some solutions to the common problems which remarried people must inevitably face.

David Hocking
Pastor of Calvary Church
Santa Ana, California

MARRYING AGAIN

Part I

The Challenges
of Remarriage

"Is it lawful for a man to divorce his wife for any cause at all?"

—Matthew 19:3

"Are you bound to a wife? Do not seek to be released. Are you released from a wife? Do not seek a wife. But if you should marry, you have not sinned; and if a virgin should marry, she has not sinned."

—1 Corinthians 7:27, 28

"A wife is bound as long as her husband lives; but if her husband is dead, she is free to be married to whom she wishes, only in the Lord."

—1 Corinthians 7:39

1

A Biblical Issue

You cannot talk about the subject of remarriage without stirring controversy among Christians. Churches disagree over the issues of divorce and remarriage, and one of the challenges we face in discussing this important subject is the matter of what the Bible teaches regarding it. It is a biblical issue!

In the fall of 1981, a seminar was held in Grand Rapids, Michigan, on the subject of divorce. Several scholars were invited to this seminar, the purpose of which was to find some agreement on the biblical material regarding divorce. After several papers and hours of discussion, the result was that there was no agreement among Bible teachers regarding this matter!

In my ministry in the local church, I must deal with the subject of divorce and remarriage. We have found that people want answers. They sincerely want to know what the Bible teaches on these subjects. They are very much aware that believers disagree over these issues and, frequently, have been deeply hurt by the attitudes and policies of churches, schools, and individuals.

The basic question has remained the same: *Do we have a biblical right to divorce or remarry?* No matter how it is phrased, that's the basic problem. Does the Bible permit divorce and remarriage under certain conditions? Some say "no" and others say "yes" and some, frankly, do not want to answer or deal with the problem. They tell the people to go somewhere else for an answer.

Remarried couples have openly expressed to me their feelings about the way the average Christian treats them. They are viewed with suspicion, and their ability to serve God effectively is continually questioned. Often, they are not allowed to serve in any leadership position in the church or to teach in the Sunday School classes of the church. They definitely cannot be considered for the pastorate or mission field. Regarded as "second-class" Christians, they are hurt and often deeply offended. You have to see this problem from their side in order to appreciate the heartache they have experienced.

I think it's time to bring the so-called "biblical issue" regarding divorce and remarriage out in the open for all to see. It is a problem. The interpretations of the divorce and remarriage passages in the Bible go from one extreme to another, depending upon whose book you have read, or whose sermon you have heard.

I would like to deal with four basic questions that people constantly ask about divorce and remarriage. They are:

1. Does the Bible permit divorce and remarriage under certain circumstances?
2. Is every divorce a sin?
3. What if your divorce was wrong?
4. When is it right to remarry?

There are, of course, many other questions that could be asked, but I prefer to deal with what people are saying rather than what the scholars would discuss (not neglecting the importance of serious study).

Does the Bible Permit Divorce and Remarriage Under Certain Circumstances?

Yes and no. It depends on the circumstances.

When Bob Younger called me one day to have lunch with him, I wasn't prepared for what he was going to tell me. He said that he and his wife were not getting along and that his wife had filed for a divorce. She told Bob: "I don't want to live with you anymore. I want you to pack your suitcase and get out!" She would not listen to him when he tried to discuss it with her.

I asked Bob: "Have you given her any cause for doing what she is doing?" He said: "The only thing I can think of is that affair I had about two years ago. She says that the Bible gives her the right to divorce me because of my immorality. Is that true?"

What I told Bob at lunch that day, I have repeated many times before and since. I opened my Bible and began to show him what the Bible teaches. I don't have the answers myself. Like you, I must turn to the Bible for help. I realize that Christians disagree over the meaning of many passages, but that shouldn't stop us from trying to study this issue. The Bible is for all of us, and not just the scholars.

Moses wrote the Book of Deuteronomy over three thousand years ago, and divorces were occurring in his time. He wrote a few verses about it, and seems to be regulating the practice. There's no command to divorce in what he says. Let's take a closer look.

> When a man takes a wife and marries her, and it happens that she finds no favor in his eyes because he has found some indecency in her, and he writes her a certificate of divorce and puts it in her hand

and sends her out from his house, and she leaves his house and goes and becomes another man's wife, and if the latter husband turns against her and writes her a certificate of divorce and puts it in her hand and sends her out of his house, or if the latter husband dies who took her to be his wife, then her former husband who sent her away is not allowed to take her again to be his wife, since she has been defiled; for that is an abomination before the Lord, and you shall not bring sin on the land which the Lord your God gives you as an inheritance.

—Deuteronomy 24:1–4

When this man gave his wife a "certificate of divorce" it was because he found some "indecency" in her. The question is, "What is the meaning of indecency?" In terms of Hebrew grammar and usage, there is not much to go on. The phrase "some indecency" is used for bowel movements in one passage, but aside from that, we are not really sure to what it refers.

The Pharisees of Jesus' day tried to trick Him on this question when they asked (Matthew 19:3; Mark 10:2): "Is it lawful for a man to divorce his wife for any cause at all?" They interpreted the phrase "some indecency" in Deuteronomy 24:1 as being for "any cause at all." The answer of Jesus is most enlightening (Matthew 19:8, 9):

Because of your hardness of heart, Moses permitted you to divorce your wives; but from the beginning it has not been this way. And I say to you, whoever divorces his wife, except for immorality, and marries another woman commits adultery.

Notice that Jesus did not say that Moses commanded divorce! He said that he "permitted" it. Jesus also indicated that God's original plan did not intend that people should be divorced. God wants you to stay married.

Jesus indicated that Moses gave permission for the children of

Israel to divorce and that the reason why people were getting divorces was "hardness of heart." Instead of forgiving each other and trying to keep their marriages together, they were stubborn and selfish.

Jesus also said that one thing breaks the marital bond and allows the innocent party to remarry. It is "immorality." This word refers to all kinds of sexual immorality, including adultery, incest, homosexuality, or bestiality. Does this then mean that Jesus was interpreting the Deuteronomy 24:1 phrase, "some indecency," as sexual immorality? The answer to that is "no!" He could not have meant that because those sexual sins in the Book of Deuteronomy were punishable by death, not a bill of divorcement.

The teaching of Jesus on what breaks up a marriage and allows for a remarriage is in addition to information we find in the Book of Deuteronomy. Moses was not commanding or encouraging divorce. He simply gave instructions on what to do about the divorces that were being granted in his day (for causes other than sexual immorality). We do not know what the meaning of "some indecency" is, but we do know that "hardness of heart" was behind it. A man has a "hard heart" when he decides to divorce his wife. The one exception would be in the case of sexual immorality. Under the Old Testament law, a person guilty of immorality could be stoned to death. Under New Testament teaching, that same person could be divorced. However, neither option is required. A third option is to apply God's forgiveness.

A very hurt young man talked to me recently about his wife's affair with one of his so-called friends. This young man is a good Bible student and had plans to go into the ministry in the future. He felt very righteous as he said to me, "I know I have the right to divorce her and marry someone else." I replied, "Is that the way God handles us when we sin against Him?" I reminded him of the example of Hosea in the Old Testament; Hosea repeatedly forgave his wife for her constant adulteries. God used this example to show us how He deals with us; He forgives and accepts us back into His loving arms. Fortunately for this young man, he responded well to the Bible's teaching on forgiveness and he and his wife are back together again.

Is Every Divorce a Sin?

After I had finished a message on divorce and how God can bring people back together again, a lady confronted me with these words: "You forgot one thing, Pastor! You forgot to remind us that every divorce is a sin!" I know that most people believe that, but I was not sure myself, so I decided to study it further.

An amazing thing occurred to me while I was studying the subject of divorce in the Bible. Divorce is nowhere listed as a sin in the many lists of sins in the Bible. I reasoned that these lists were only summaries and not complete. But that one point began to work on me. Why is it that most churches hold divorce to be more serious than other sins? And, why is it never mentioned as a sin?

In some passages we could argue that certain kinds of divorce are described as being wrong. Let's make a brief list:

1. *Divorce in Malachi 2.*

Malachi 2:16 says, "For I hate divorce," and this comes from the lips of the Lord. The divorces which God hates in that context are those in which Israel divorced their wives and married "daughters of foreign gods" (v. 11). Five times in Malachi 2:10–16 we find the phrase "deal treacherously." It certainly indicates wrongdoing on the part of those getting such divorces.

2. *Divorce in Matthew 5:32 and 19:9 and Mark 10:11, 12.*

As discussed earlier, Jesus indicates that divorcing your wife or husband without the grounds of sexual immorality is not only wrong, but causes you to commit adultery when you remarry.

3. *Divorce in 1 Corinthians 7:12, 13.*

This passage deals with a believer who is married to an unbeliever. If the unbeliever wants to continue to live with the believer, the believer is instructed not to get a divorce.

But, is every divorce a sin? These three examples listed above are certainly wrong. But what about divorces based on sexual immorality? Didn't Jesus argue that this would be an exception? What about the case of Joseph and Mary? When Mary was pregnant and Joseph found out, he wanted to "put her away secretly." That means that he wanted to divorce her, and do it as quietly as possible so as not to embarrass Mary any further. Matthew 1:19 calls Joseph "a righteous man" and commends him for his actions. Could the Bible do that if all divorce was wrong? Of course not.

The Apostle Paul taught in 1 Corinthians 7:15:

> Yet if the unbelieving one leaves, let him leave; the brother or the sister is not under bondage in such cases, but God has called us to peace.

Though Christians disagree sharply over the meaning of this verse, one thing is clear: the believer is not being condemned under these circumstances. You might argue that the believer did not get the divorce; but regardless of who obtained the divorce, the result is that the believer is "not under bondage." Some people say that the phrase "not under bondage" means that the believer is not obligated to stay with the unbeliever. However, isn't that already obvious? The unbeliever has left! Many Christians believe that the phrase "not under bondage" refers to the matter of remarriage. If this is the case, then the believer is free to remarry when the unbeliever has left.

In summary, many divorces are clearly wrong, but not all divorces. Divorces based on sexual immorality and the willing departure of an unbelieving partner cannot be categorically denied to believers. In Jeremiah 3:8, God gave Israel a bill of divorce because of her spiritual adulteries. Since God cannot sin, it seems impossible to argue that all divorce is sin.

What If Your Divorce Was Wrong?

I had just finished teaching on divorce in one of our marriage seminars when a lovely lady in her forties approached me and wanted to ask a question. She said, "My divorce was clearly wrong. I was selfish and guilty of many things. My husband never remarried. What should I do?" I encouraged her to confess her sin to the Lord, and to her former husband, and seek his forgiveness. I challenged her to trust God to change her husband's heart and ask him if he would consider getting back together again. She seemed excited to do so.

No sooner had this lady left, than a second woman in her twenties asked me this question: "I divorced my husband because I was involved with another man who I thought would marry me. He didn't, and chose someone else to marry. My former husband has now remarried. Can we get back together again?" The two examples were similar, but different in one major point—remarriage. When your partner has remarried after your divorce, I do not believe you should try to get back together again. I base my belief on what Deuteronomy 24:1–4 teaches. However, some Bible teachers would allow such a thing if the reason for the divorce was not sexual immorality. Their point would be that without the grounds of sexual immorality, any remarriage after a divorce would be wrong, and, according to Jesus, would result in a state of adultery. So, in their view, it would be possible to break up the second marriage, and return to the former partner. They believe that what is necessary is simply to forgive the continuous adultery of the former partner, based on their belief that the remarriage was not valid in the eyes of God.

However, I feel that the emotional and psychological adjustments caused by divorce and remarriage make it extremely difficult for the original partners to restore the relationship that they once had. There may be exceptions to this, but as a general rule, it simply does not work. I think it would be better to realize that God has a reason for His restrictions in Deuteronomy 24:1–4.

I hate to see grown men cry, but that's exactly what Ted was doing in my office. He said, "Pastor, I should never have divorced my wife! I had no reasons other than the fact that we couldn't get along with each other. We were always at each other's throat! Now that my wife is dead, I can't sleep at nights knowing that my divorce was wrong. Is it too late for me to do anything about it now?" Obviously, there was nothing we could do about straightening things out with his former wife, but Ted himself could get straightened out with the Lord. I urged him to confess his sin and recommit himself to God's standards in the Word of God. I told him that no sin was too great for God to forgive. He made a beautiful commitment to the Lord, and a wonderful peace came over him as he learned to accept God's forgiveness and love.

No matter what caused your divorce, nothing is outside of the ability of God to forgive! How sad that many people refuse to acknowledge that their divorces were based on sin, and not righteous grounds! Why is it that people are so hesitant to admit that their divorces were wrong? Why do people struggle so hard to justify and defend what they have done? Is it not the pride of our hearts? Is it not our failure to believe and accept God's forgiveness and cleansing? Do we not often believe that our future ministry will be destroyed if we admit that we are guilty of wrongdoing in our divorce?

I argued with Bill for quite a long time regarding his divorce. He tried to explain it, but the longer he talked, the more he realized that he had no "grounds" for what he had done. It was so hard for him to admit that his divorce was wrong. He knew that if he admitted that, he would have to go to his former wife and apologize and seek her forgiveness and try to win her back. Finally, he blurted out, "If I do admit that it was sin on my part, will the church keep reminding me of it in the future?" That was his great concern because he had such a desire to be a leader in our church. I told him then as I tell you now—when we confess and repent of our sins, God forgives and cleanses everything. I assured him that our church would not bring up this matter against him in the future if he truly confessed his sin and repented of it.

When Is It Right to Remarry?

One of the most frequently asked questions in the counseling room is "Am I free to remarry?" Of course, some people don't bother to ask! They just go ahead and get married again without considering the problems they may encounter in the future. Believe it or not, many remarried couples ask the question about their own marriage. Even though years have passed, they still want to know about their so-called "biblical rights."

One couple who asked to see me about a very important problem took me completely by surprise. The husband was a leader in another church and had been active in many different kinds of ministry over quite a number of years. His wife played the piano for several Sunday School classes and was a good Bible teacher in one of our home Bible fellowship groups. This couple seemed happily married and, as far as I knew at the time, had no past problems that would hinder their present ministries. The trouble began when the husband applied to a theological seminary. He was interested in becoming a pastor and wanted one day to have his own church. On the application form, the school asked about his marital background, forcing him to admit to a previous divorce and to declare that he was now remarried. I did not know that he was divorced and remarried and I don't think any of their church members knew about it either. The school turned down his application because of his divorce and remarriage.

In my office he said, "Pastor, why do they not accept divorced and remarried people?" I suggested that some divorces and remarriages were clearly wrong according to the Scriptures. He replied, "But I was divorced by my first wife who ran off with another man and married him." He continued by saying, "We were young and foolish, and knew very little about how to make a marriage what God wants it to be. Besides, I was not a Christian at the time." I asked, "When did you become a Christian?" He answered, "After I was married to my present wife. We've been happily married now for fifteen years."

In spite of my attempts to persuade that school that this man had valid reasons for his divorce and remarriage and that he now was demonstrating a habit of life that made him "a one-woman man," the school stuck to its policy of not accepting divorced or remarried people as students. I realized then as I do now that Christians disagree strongly over the issues of divorce and remarriage. It definitely affects the ministry of those who have experienced divorce and remarriage.

My advice to this couple was to seek another school which would be more open to the training of divorced and remarried people for full-time ministry. They did so, and after several years of study, he is now a pastor of his own church. They seem happy and God is blessing their ministry.

Whether we like it or not, churches and schools that are committed to biblical authority do not always agree as to what the Bible teaches concerning divorce and remarriage. They want to do what is right, and sometimes they think that encouraging divorced and remarried people to study for the ministry violates the qualifications set down in the Bible for ministers.

These views affect divorced and remarried people who try to serve their local churches in various capacities of leadership and ministry. Some churches will not allow any divorced or remarried people to be elders or deacons. Some do not allow divorced or remarried people to teach Sunday School or home Bible studies. These viewpoints have a tendency to drive divorced and remarried people away from our churches. The hurts can continue for several years and the results are damaging to Christian life and growth.

To be quite honest, my own ministry used to have these restrictions concerning divorced and remarried people. Today I do not. In my opinion, it is possible to be divorced and not be guilty of any wrongdoing. I believe that the right of remarriage is always granted to someone whose divorce was permitted by God.

A sad story was related to me by a businessman in his thirties whom I had met in a local restaurant. He had heard me speak on our daily radio broadcast and recognized my voice in the booth next to where he was sitting. He joined me for a cup of coffee and told me the story of his divorce. He was convinced he had righteous grounds for it, for his wife had left him for another man. After some years, he met a lovely Christian lady and before many months passed, they wanted to get married. He went to see his pastor and told him about his past divorce. The pastor said, "John, there is no way that I would marry you. Just because your divorce was based on your wife's unfaithfulness, that does not give you the right to remarry." John was upset, and said, "But my former wife has already remarried." His pastor said, "She is living in adultery. God does not recognize her marriage. You must wait for her to come back to you. It is not right for you to get married again." In spite of John's attempts to defend his position, the pastor of his church refused to marry him. Both he and his new lady friend left that church and joined another church and were married in it.

But John was still bothered about the whole situation, and asked me my opinion. I said, "John, the Bible gives you permission to divorce and to remarry. I don't know how many times you tried to forgive your wife and win her back. I'm supposing that you tried to do that. Forgiveness is always the best way." John said, "I tried many times, but she was determined." I said, "When did you start dating your present wife?" He answered, "Not until my former wife had remarried." I shook his hand and said, "Then you have nothing to worry about. Your conscience is clear." He thanked me and seemed relieved.

When Is It Wrong to Remarry?

This is often a better question to ask yourself than "Do I have the right to remarry?" You may have the right, and yet it may be wrong for you. One of our church members talked with me about his desire to be remarried. He said, "The one thing that bothers me is that I don't have a clear conscience about my relationship with Janice." Janice was his former wife; she had divorced him, but had not remarried. I said, "Bill, you have no business getting remarried until this issue is resolved! You better try to get reconciled with Janice before any more thoughts fill your mind about remarriage." I then shared three reasons why it is wrong to remarry.

1. *It is wrong to remarry if your past problems have not been resolved.* What caused your divorce? Has your former partner remarried? Have you tried to be reconciled with your former

mate who has not remarried? Have you confessed and repented of your actions that led to your divorce when you had no biblical grounds? In speaking about true repentance, Paul wrote in 2 Corinthians 7:11 that it includes the "avenging of wrong." He wrote, "In everything you demonstrated yourselves to be innocent in the matter." Is that true of your past?

Bob had been divorced twice, but had never faced his problem. He was guilty of insufficient commitment to his marital partner. He had an eye for other women and always seemed to find someone else who was more attractive or more capable of meeting his needs. The girl he wanted this time was more discerning than the others. She wanted to know why he had failed in his two previous marriages. Bob was uncomfortable with her questions. He kept insisting that if she really loved him she would take him as he is. She decided that she deserved more. She wanted a strong commitment from him. She refused to marry him until he would deal with his problem. He was too proud, and decided to date someone else. He was married soon, and that marriage ended tragically in divorce.

If you have not faced the past, seeking to resolve past conflicts and wrong decisions, then do so immediately. Don't carry those problems into another marriage. You're not only hurting yourself, but your new partner.

2. *It is wrong to remarry if you do not have a clear conscience about doing so.* So many people pay little attention to this problem, only to suffer because of it. If you are in doubt about it, then don't do it. Even if your friends are pushing you into getting remarried, don't do it unless your doubts have departed.

Romans 14:22, 23 gives us this principle:

The faith which you have, have as your own conviction before God. Happy is he who does not condemn himself in what he approves. But he who doubts is condemned if he eats, because his eating is not from faith; and whatever is not from faith is sin.

We are not talking about the doubts you may have over your ability to make someone happy, or the fear you have that you might fail again. We are talking about doubting whether this remarriage is right for you. If you are not sure you are doing the right thing, then it is always better to wait.

Susan James was in love with Barry Hensley and really looking forward to marrying him. It was to be his third marriage and her second. Everything seemed resolved about their past marriages and divorces, but one thing continued to bother her. In a premarital counseling session with one of our pastors, Susan said, "I'm not sure Barry is a real believer!" She went on to say that her Christian friends told her not to worry about it because it could be a case of a carnal Christian. After all, a believer can look great the day before marriage, and like a carnal Christian the day after. Susan wasn't satisfied with that. She asked, "Does it matter, Pastor, if I'm not sure about Barry's faith in the Lord?" She already knew in her heart that it did. He replied, "Susan, you had better confront Barry directly about his faith in Christ." A few days later she did. She called the pastor on the phone and said, "Pastor, he became very upset and accused me of trying to be superspiritual." She was encouraged to wait and not get married until this issue was resolved.

Time reveals a great deal. Susan decided to wait, and Barry got mad and broke the engagement. Within two months, he married someone else, and within three months after his marriage, he was divorced again. Susan was glad that she waited.

A good friend, Andrew Johnson, is a tremendous example to people who have been divorced and are seeking help regarding remarriage. When his wife divorced him, he was deeply hurt. He still loved her and the children. He did two things that today have given him the confidence he has before God and his family. One, he did not date anyone else either before the divorce was final (during their days of separation) or after it was signed. Today he has a clear conscience because of that commitment. Secondly, he kept his responsibility as a father to his children, both in terms of financial support and care, as well as his time and discipline. When his wife moved from the Midwest to California with the children, he quit his job and moved also, so that he could be near his children and be there when his family needed him. He did not pressure his wife during all of this time. She seemed to appreciate his help, although she finally married another man. When his wife remarried, according to his testimony, God removed the strong love he had for her from his heart. After seeking counsel from mature believers, he began to pray for God to give him another wife whom he could love. Today, he is happily married and God is blessing his ministry to others.

The lesson to be learned from this man's testimony is the importance of waiting upon the Lord for His clear direction and will regarding the possibility of remarriage. A divorced person should not be anxious to date others until the circumstances with his/her former spouse clearly show that all hope of reconciliation is gone.

3. *It is wrong to remarry if you do not have a strong desire to do so.* Some people remarry under pressure from others. Being single is sometimes criticized by those who think that everybody should get married. Churches have been slow to recognize the single person in their ministries. One gets the feeling that you can serve the Lord better if you are married.

The Apostle Paul taught otherwise. In 1 Corinthians 7:32–35, he said:

But I want you to be free from concern. One who is unmarried is concerned about the things of the Lord, how he may please the Lord; but one who is married is concerned about the things of the world, how he may please his wife, and his interests are divided. And the woman who is unmarried, and the virgin, is concerned about the things of the Lord, that she may be holy both in body and spirit; but one who is married is concerned about the things of the world, how she may please her husband. And this I say for your own benefit; not to put a restraint upon you, but to promote what is seemly, and to secure undistracted devotion to the Lord.

Paul exalts the single state. He says that our capacity to serve the Lord is greatly increased by remaining single. To marry is not always the thing to do. It's not for everyone. If you do not have the strong desire for marriage, then consider remaining single and devoting your time and energies to the cause of Christ.

One night about ten o'clock, a friend dropped by our house and shared with my wife the pressure she was under about remarriage. She frankly did not know what to do about it. She is attractive and not yet 35 years old. Her divorce resulted from her former husband's affair with another woman whom he eventually married. She told my wife, "Carole, I don't really have a strong desire to get married, but my Christian friends are all telling me that I should. What do you think?" My wife told her not to make such a decision unless she really wanted to be remarried. She went on to explain to my wife that she did not have strong physical desires for a husband. She isn't devoid of such desires, but she said that it was not a pressure in her life. She is a very loving person, and enjoys being single. She has time to do many wonderful things for the Lord.

My wife told her, "Don't let others pressure you into marriage. Make sure that it is the Lord's will for you. If you don't have to be married, and are not desiring it right now, it is much better to remain single." She said to my wife, "Do you think I am strange for wanting to be single?" My wife assured her that such was not the case and that God has encouraged singles in the Bible and commended them for their decision to remain single and serve the Lord. She left that night (after midnight!) a relieved woman. The pressure was gone, and she was happy in the Lord.

Before you remarry, ask yourself these three basic questions:

1. Are all my past problems resolved?
2. Do I have a clear conscience about getting remarried?
3. Do I have a strong desire to be married again?

If you are already remarried, then you can't go back and do things over again. If your divorce was wrong, confess it, and repent of it. Keep building your present marriage on God's principles of love, forgiveness, and commitment. None of us can run away from the many questions which divorce and remarriage bring. They must be answered. Once that is done and you have the peace of God controlling your heart, then it's time to get on with your life. Your present marriage and family needs your attention and commitment.

Questions for Reflection

1. Does the Bible permit divorce and remarriage? If so, under what circumstances?
2. Is every divorce a sin? How do you know?
3. What should a person do if the divorce was wrong?
4. For what three reasons is it wrong to remarry?
5. Are there any past problems in your life that have not been resolved? What can you do about it? Will you?

2

The Former Partner

Feelings about your former partner depend upon a wide variety of factors. It's comparatively easy to forget a former partner with whom you spent very few years, but after many years of marriage, the memories are deep. Your feelings toward a former partner are also based upon the kind of relationship you had. If your former marriage was one bad experience, then your ability to forget and bury the past will be much easier than if your relationship was good and rewarding. The reasons for the termination of that marriage are also contributing factors to how you feel about your former partner. If your husband or wife died you will have far different feelings than those who have experienced divorce. Also, the way the divorce was handled or accepted can affect any future relationships you may have with your former partner.

The fact is, no matter what kind of relationship you had with your former partner, you must learn to deal with your memories and feelings toward that partner, especially after you are remarried.

Stop Comparing!

Les made a great mistake one day when he said to Elizabeth that she did not cook as well as his former wife. He wishes that he had never made that remark. Elizabeth prides herself on her ability to prepare delicious and nutritional meals. Les was simply thinking of a particular meal that his former wife used to make for him and in that moment of comparison failed to realize the effect his words would have upon Elizabeth. It took some time before Elizabeth got over what he had said.

Some of the most serious mistakes are made in terms of comparing physical appearance. One lady friend of ours is convinced that her husband has related to her differently since she dyed her hair the same color as his former wife. She was aware of how often he spoke of his wife's hair and its color. His present wife's hair was an opposite color and it did not seem to please him as much as the color of his former wife's hair. This issue may seem small and insignificant to some people, but it has deeply affected this couple and hindered their response to each other.

Jerry and Marge seem like a happily remarried couple. But they have just one problem which continues to rear its ugly head. Jerry's former wife had a very nice figure while Marge is average in appearance and somewhat on the thin side. She feels very insecure about Jerry's thoughts of her in comparison to his former wife. He says that he doesn't think about it often, but Marge hears his frequent references to the "great body" of his former wife. This has damaged their relationship although Jerry seems somewhat oblivious to it. He needs to learn to rejoice in the wife to whom he is now married!

Comparisons to a former partner will only damage your present relationship. Realize how destructive such comparisons can be and determine to stop doing it. One helpful thing you can do is concentrate on the positive qualities of your present partner and frequently compliment that partner. The more you praise the qualities and attributes of your present partner, the less you will compare him or her to your former partner.

It is one thing to remember your former partner; it is another thing to make comparisons. When you compare, it suggests some dissatisfaction with your present partner. Ask yourself why you are making the comparison. Is the problem still in your heart? Have you committed this matter to the Lord?

What the Remarried Say About Former Partners

I composed a series of questions about former partners and tested them out on six different couples who have been remarried. Their answers were most enlightening. My questions included:

1. Do you think much about your former partner?
2. Do you see your former partner on a regular basis?
3. Do your children ask about your former partner?
4. How does your present partner compare with your former partner?

Each couple was unique and their circumstances were very different from the others. This helped me greatly in evaluating the problems of the remarried. It is wrong, I believe, to make statements about the remarried that do not include or give consideration to such differences.

Couple No. 1—Communication Difficulties

The first couple I interviewed found it difficult to discuss issues relating to their former partners and they have made their children aware that they do not want to talk about them. That is especially hard on the children.

When I asked them whether they thought much about their former partners, the husband said, "Not much." His wife said, "No!" I got the distinct impression that they were not going to tell me much about their feelings. When I asked if they ever saw their former partners, the husband said, "Definitely not!" The wife said, "Never." Concerning the questions their children might ask about the former partners, the husband said, "We do not discuss it," and the wife said, "They have learned not to ask me anymore." Their responses here are not good. The children need to be dealt with honestly and lovingly.

My question dealing with comparing the present partner with the former one generated some pretty strong reactions. The husband said, "No comparison! My present wife makes me forget my first wife!" The wife said, "My husband makes my former partner look sick!" This couple is filled with bitterness about their former marriages. They seem to use the tactic of not discussing it in order to avoid the hard reality of what they feel about them. I encouraged them to discuss their feelings with a Christian counselor and to allow their children to ask any questions they want without feeling pressure or anger.

Couple No. 2—Emotional Ties

This couple has three children living with them. One belongs to the wife, the other two to the husband. Thoughts about the former partner evidently do not enter this husband's mind. The wife, however, made this interesting remark: "Sometimes I like to remember the things we used to do that were good. Most of the time I just want to forget about him (former husband)." This wife misses her first husband, but has a hard time admitting it.

She had a lot of fun with her first husband that seems to be lacking in her second marriage.

In answer to my question about seeing the former partner from time to time, the husband said, "I stay as far away from her as I possibly can!" The wife said, "No, but from time to time I wish that I could see him and find out how he is getting along." This wife needs to deal with her emotional ties to her first husband.

Concerning the children's questions, the husband responded, "I don't want them to think about her, but they do ask." The wife opened up at this point and said, "I have one child and my husband has two. My child talks to me quite a bit about her daddy. She has a hard time relating to my present husband as well as his two children. They are older and she feels left out much of the time. To be quite honest, she seems to really miss her daddy." Of course, that last statement is also true of this wife. This family is under quite a bit of tension and pressure. They would profit from doing more things together. The husband needs to loosen up a bit and enjoy times with his family and his wife in particular.

In making a comparison, the husband did not want to think about it, but the wife responded: "We had some good times (first husband). My present husband is a fine man. My first husband was more fun at times. My present husband is more reliable."

Couple No. 3—Guilt Feelings

Because the wife had no children by her former marriage, and her husband definitely cared about the children of his former marriage, both of these partners were filled with guilt. The wife feels like she can't measure up and wonders if she can satisfy her husband's needs. He can't forget his former family and misses them terribly.

Concerning thoughts of the former partner, he said that he thought of his former wife "all the time." He said that he talks with her frequently. He added, "I made some real mistakes in my relationship with her. I take all the blame for our divorce. I know I hurt her very much." The wife had little to say about her former husband, but usually referred to the feelings of her present husband. "His first wife was good to him," she says. When I asked about comparing your present partner to your former partner, she said, "My present husband is definitely a family man. It's nice at times. My former husband and I had no children."

This woman suffers from his guilt though he is not aware of it. She senses that she is not the woman that his first wife was to him. They are good friends (present partners) and he enjoys her company very much. However, he really misses his children. He needs to stop calling his former wife as frequently as he does. He still seems emotionally attached to his first wife and family, and because of the guilt he feels, he's having a difficult time adjusting to his present wife. She knows what he feels but isn't sure what to do about it. She needs much more affection from him and also wants to know that he is truly satisfied with her.

Couple No. 4—Hostile Attitudes

This couple manifests a common problem among the remarried. Our attitudes are often hostile and bitter toward the former partner. When I asked about any thoughts they might have about former partners, the husband said, "Only when she calls and wants something." The wife had a different attitude. She said, "I worry about him (former husband) at times since he did not remarry. I wonder if he's taking care of himself. He's very undisciplined." Her feelings were mixed. She became angry when discussing her former husband's undisciplined habits, but she still manifested concern for him since he did not remarry. She felt responsible for him. She openly shared that she would feel better if he were remarried.

This wife is not aggressive and is not sure how to talk with her new husband. She feels guilty for not having been able to meet her first husband's needs. She "mothered" her first husband, and now that he is alone and hasn't remarried, she feels responsible. Her present husband is an uptight person who has very hostile feelings toward his first wife. He quickly refers to her "nagging." When I asked him to compare his former wife with his present one, he responded: "My first wife drove me crazy, nagging me all the time. What I like about my present wife is that she doesn't argue with me about every little thing. She seems to accept me like I am. I don't know why my present wife's husband left her. He never saw her potential I guess. He didn't like her because she wasn't aggressive, but I'll tell you—that's what I like about her. I had enough of the other type!"

This husband has difficulty handling his former wife when she comes to pick up the kids. He can't seem to keep quiet. Whenever he speaks, the hostility pours out. He tries to justify his actions and feelings. He wants to believe that his children agree with him about their mother. This man needs to learn how to handle these difficult situations in his life and to get rid of his bitterness. He also needs to spend time building up his present wife. He seems quite selfish and is assuming that her needs are being met.

Couple No. 5—Deep Hurts

This couple had a very difficult time during the interview. Obviously, they have both been hurt deeply. They have tried to console each other but have not really experienced God's love and forgiveness toward their former partners. They have three children living at home (two of his, one of hers), and none of them are relating well to what has happened.

My first question about thoughts of the former partner brought this response from the husband: "Sometimes I wonder if she's happy with the man she wanted instead of me." The wife said, "Both my husband and I were hurt by our partners leaving us for other people. Naturally, there are scars we would like to forget. But it's hard to forget."

When I asked if they see their former partners from time to time, he said, "I see her from a distance, but she never talks to me." She said, "No, and frankly I don't want to after he did what he did."

Both of them opened up quite a bit when I asked about the children's questions concerning former partners. He said, "They often ask me why mother left. When I first told them that she wanted another man for a husband, they got mad at me, insinuating that I must have done something to cause her to leave. No doubt I had problems. But the fact is, she left me for a man with whom she was having an affair. I don't know if the children have ever been able to accept this, although they seem to relate well to my present wife."

She responded, "I know my husband is having trouble with his two kids. They don't relate to me as well as he thinks. I think they still wonder why his former wife, their mother, left him for another man. I have one child who is in college, and one at home. My oldest son seems to understand that his dad was messing around with this woman and finally married her. He doesn't seem bitter, but then you never know. My younger son is still hurt over his dad leaving us. It's hard for him to talk about it."

When I asked about comparing his present partner with his former partner, he said: "My present wife was really hurt about her husband leaving her, so she has had some difficulty responding to me and trusting me. I know what she feels. My first wife was really sexy, flirting all the time. It made me mad, but she wouldn't stop. I guess the real difference is that my first wife could never get enough sexual satisfaction from our relationship, but my present wife is more contented. Sometimes I wish she wanted sex more often, but then I remember what happened to my first wife, so I'm kind of glad she doesn't."

His wife had this to say in comparing her former husband to her present husband: "My first husband was 'Mr. Macho.' He had an eye for other women. He wanted sex every night (it seemed!). Other women were always flirting with him. He is good-looking and had a great build. I think I knew for a long time that he was playing around, but I had a hard time admitting it. I wasn't surprised when he left me for another woman. She was totally different from me. She was sexy and provocative and he liked that. My present husband is more responsible and doesn't demand things that I think are questionable."

The deep hurts of this couple will not go away easily, but with proper counseling, it can happen. More time must be spent by this couple and their children dealing with what has happened and why. The children also need to understand God's love and forgiveness without excusing what their former parents have done. When the parents get rid of their hurts, then the children will be more relaxed and understanding. Some attention needs to be given to the desire for sex as it relates to their past and present needs.

Couple No. 6—Complete Satisfaction

This couple was pure joy! Both of their former partners had died. There were no divorces to contend with, and no unhappy experiences in the past. They both were quite comfortable with my questions and had no difficulty talking about their former partners.

To my first question, the husband said, "I miss her very much. After she died, I never thought I would remarry, but God has been so good to me and given me a very understanding wife whose husband also died." The wife said, "My former husband was a wonderful man. Yes, I think about him a lot. However, God gave me a wonderful man who understands how I feel. We both have good memories, but have learned how to help each other."

Concerning the questions any of their children might have, the husband said, "Our children are grown up now. They are married and have families of their own. They speak often of their mother, and it's obvious that we all miss her." His wife responded, "My children are married, and when we get together (usually on holidays), we sometimes remember the good times we enjoyed with their father. We are all thankful that he is with the Lord, but we still miss him. The children relate well to my present husband. The Lord has been good to us."

I was thrilled with this interview and most interested, as it was moving along, to see how they would respond to the question of comparing their former mate to their present one. The wife spoke up first: "It's very hard to compare two good men. I have much to be thankful for and each is special to me. My present husband and I are really happy." He added, "Both of my wives have been very special ladies. They seem quite similar to me at times. My first wife and I had many wonderful years together. But my present wife and I are really enjoying each other. Frankly, it's a hard question to answer. Both wives have been all that I could ever hope for!"

What an example of God's love and maturity this couple presents! It shows us the difference between death and divorce. They can communicate freely and openly about their former partners with no suspicions or jealousies. They have their memories and are protective of each other's feelings. They are both complimentary about their former mates, yet have learned to love each other as deeply as they loved their partners who died. What a testimony! What more could I possibly add? My thanks to all of these couples, and especially couple No. 6!

The Impact of Death

It is common for people who have been married for many years to believe that when their partners die, they will never marry again. Some go so far as to promise their mates that they will never remarry. Perhaps it is not surprising to see people re-marry after having experienced a long and happy marriage with a partner who died, but it is at least difficult for most people to adjust to the new partner if their relationship with the first part-ner was a close one.

Statistics reveal that most people will remarry after their part-ner dies if given the opportunity. A certain amount of time must pass before an individual is emotionally ready to enter another marital relationship, but the desire for companionship is power-ful, and the loneliness can often seem unbearable.

One particular lady that we know was very strong in her feel-ings that she would never marry again. She had enjoyed over thirty years of happy experiences with her husband, and now that he was dead, she felt that she would betray him by marrying again. However, within a few short months, the loneliness she felt became too much for her. She talked with several people about what she should do. She was still very attractive, and felt that she needed a husband. Some of her friends were shocked that she wanted to marry again. She felt more guilty after listen-ing to them and their feelings about her former husband. I as-sured her that the Bible gave her permission to remarry, but she had to settle the issue in her heart. I encouraged her to resolve her problem before marrying again. That's exactly what she did, and after a year and a half she married a wonderful man whose wife had died about four years previous to their meeting each other.

Paul encouraged widows to remain single if possible (1 Corinthians 7:8, 9), but to marry again if they did not have control over their sexual desires. Some people still have strong desires for a companion, and it is not a sin to remarry after your partner dies.

A friend's wife was dying of cancer, and he was spending every moment he could with her during the last few weeks of her life. About one week before she died, she told him that she knew his needs quite well and believed that he should get married again. He was embarrassed by such talk and told her that he did not want to discuss it. But she insisted. She even advised him to marry one of their close friends whose husband had died about a year previous. She had confidence in that woman, and believed that she and her husband would be able to have a happy marriage. About six months after his wife died, he married the very woman whom his wife had wanted him to marry. After several years, they are still quite happy and can speak freely and openly about their former partners without suspicion or hesitation. Their relationship has taught many others about how a remarriage situation can deal with former relationships.

It is not always right for a widow or widower to be remarried. If there is no pressure from within to do so, then such a person should never succumb to the pressure of others. We have seen some unhappy marriages that have resulted from such pressure. One lady was pressured by her lady friends to marry a certain man when she really did not want to be remarried. She has lived to regret her decision. One man continued to pressure a widow lady to marry him. He drove her crazy by his constant attempts to persuade her. She finally gave in to his advances though in her heart she did not want to marry again. She suffers much today because of that decision. Her remarriage has not been happy and fulfilling.

The Problem of Suicide

The suicide of a mate is perhaps the most difficult and trying experience a marital partner can have. We have seen the suffering and anguish which suicide brings. It is never easy to overcome. The guilt you feel is tremendous. You keep wondering where you failed, and whether there was something you could have done to prevent the suicide. This guilt can continue for several years unless you learn about and accept God's sovereignty and forgiveness.

Suicides are not discussed much in Christian circles. The attitudes of Christians are not clear on this matter. All suicides are certainly selfish acts, but Christians disagree on several matters relating to them. Can a Christian commit suicide? Does suicide prevent you from going to heaven? Is it an unpardonable sin? The fact is that suicides (and attempts to commit suicide) are much more common than people realize. There is always an effort to hide the facts and explain the death by other means. It is most difficult to face and live with the fact that your partner committed suicide. It is quite a burden to relate to people after it happens. What do you say? You keep wondering what other people are thinking. Do they blame you for what your partner did? Christians need to show much love and understanding to friends whose partners have committed suicide. We must stop suspecting or insinuating that these people have failed because of what their partners have done.

After a suicide has occurred, a person is reluctant to marry the partner who remains. It takes a loving and sensitive person to rebuild the confidence and security of one who lost a former partner by suicide.

The Devastation of Divorce

In some respects, divorce is like death. The sense of loss is comparable, and in many cases, the emotional adjustment is similar. It hurts no matter what the reason for it. The relationship to the former partner varies greatly, depending on the circumstances. If your partner left you for another person, you will have one set of feelings; if you left your partner for someone else, you will have another kind of emotional response.

One of the most common feelings a person experiences toward a partner who divorced him or her is *resentment.* You begin to ask, "Who does he think he is?" Or, you say, "I don't deserve what she did to me!" It's hard to get over what you feel in this regard. When you think of your former partner you become upset. Some people get ulcers just thinking about it.

One couple we know has been having trouble in their marriage because of the wife's response to her former husband. She sees him and his new wife frequently. He left her for this woman. Her feelings of bitterness and resentment are so strong they are affecting her relationship to her present husband. She can't seem to forgive her former husband for what he did. Her present husband suffers because of it.

One lady friend of ours is finding it difficult to relate to her present husband because he continually refers to the "good points" of his former wife. The two women have to look at each other every week because they attend the same church.

Questions for Reflection

1. What are some of the common feelings that people have toward their former partners?
2. What issues need to be settled in terms of your former partner?
3. What should be said to your children about your former partner?

4. What factors caused some of these couples interviewed to be negative toward their former partners?
5. Why do you think that the last couple (p. 43) was so happy?
6. After reading what these six couples had to say about their former partners, what did you learn about your own feelings?
7. What impact does death have upon remarriage? What about suicide?

3

The Stepchildren

The real trouble among the remarried does not lie with resolving past conflicts relating to divorce or the right of remarriage. Even the delicate situations dealing with former partners do not bring the greatest trials. The real trouble, according to many remarried couples, is the raising and handling of children who are not their own. No problem seems as great as that of your stepchildren. Few burdens can be heavier than a stepchild who refuses to respond to you.

Where Does It Start?

The trouble begins in the heart of the child who must cope with the breakup of the family. It starts the first day that the child learns that his parents are not going to live together anymore. That news is devastating to a child, especially when it comes without warning.

Andy Wellington and his wife, Mary, had been having difficulties for several years, but they did a pretty good job of keeping their differences hidden from their children. They finally decided to divorce. When Andy told his young son (only eight years old), the boy ran out of the house and down the street, crying his heart out. When Mary tried to tell her little five-year-old girl that she and Andy would not be living together anymore, the little girl could not believe it. She kept asking, "But, why, Mommie, why?" Mary could not keep back the tears. Every explanation she tried did not seem to help. When Andy finally caught up to his son and brought him back to the house, he refused to listen to any of their explanations. He just went to his room and kept crying.

About six months later, Andy decided to remarry, and he asked Mary if he could have his son. They agreed that Mary would keep the little girl, and Andy, the boy. From the first day that Andy's son met his new mother, he hated her. He refused to talk with her, and would not call her "Mother." Andy was so frustrated over his boy's response, he did not know what to do. He tried discipline, but the boy got worse. The boy's grades in school were dropping rapidly, and he began to get into lots of trouble. He was involved in several fights at school and in his new neighborhood. Andy was desperate, and came to see me one day about his problem. At the time, I did not know the background. When I heard what had happened, I was not surprised. Andy's son was experiencing deep bitterness and feelings of rejection that he could not handle. Andy and his new wife were only concerned about the surface problems in the boy's life, and had failed to deal with his deep hurt. It started the first day Andy tried to tell him that he and Mary were going to get a divorce.

It took almost two years before Andy's son would begin to relate to his stepmother. Today, he is a teenager and the emotional scars are still there, but he is growing in his relationship to Christ, and learning more and more about God's love and forgiveness.

No matter what changes take place in the heart of the stepchild, the emotional hurt and damage is there. Parents who take a child's response to a divorce lightly are apt to find a difficult situation when the child is asked to respond properly to the stepparent.

What Can Be Done?

Many remarried couples are going through the struggles of dealing with stepchildren who have deep feelings of rejection and harbor growing bitterness toward their stepparents. They wonder: What can be done to alleviate this difficult situation?

For one thing, if you are a stepparent, don't ignore the hurts in the heart of your stepchild. It may be a hard trial for you to bear, but you are an adult! It is much more difficult for your stepchild to adjust than for you. Put yourself in the shoes of your stepchild and encourage that child to share the hurts without feeling guilty or experiencing condemnation.

John Sisler could not control his anger toward his son, Robert, who was thirteen years old and was being asked to accept John's new wife as his own mother. Robert was still pretty upset over the divorce of his father from his mother. His mother had remarried, but did not want Robert due to the three stepchildren she inherited by her remarriage. Robert felt rejected by his mother. When his dad remarried, he found it hard to relate to his new mother, Alice. Alice called me one day about John's anger. She knew that Robert was struggling with his relationship to her, and she seemed to understand and was willing to work it out in time. But John's impatience was becoming a serious problem. She said on the phone that day, "Pastor, John is trying to force

Robert to call me 'Mother,' and to obey me as if I were his real mother. He thinks his anger is going to convince Robert. But I think it's getting worse, not better."

A few days later I talked with John. He admitted his anger but also shared his frustrations with the whole problem. I encouraged him to let his son share freely and openly with him about his feelings. I said, "John, you must let your son know that you love him deeply and that you want to help him with his feelings." His son needed his father's encouragement very much. In time, this situation began to improve because of John's willingness to listen, and to help his son walk through the situation and to see God's perspective of things.

Next to the need of understanding your child's feelings of hurt, I would emphasize the importance of listening to his side of the story. The child may have some deep resentment toward you for what the child perceives as your failure to make the former marriage work. Be open and honest about what happened and relate it to the Word of God and what should be done now about it. Don't try to defend yourself or justify your mistakes. Your child needs to know that you are truthful and that you also need God's help and strength. Let your child know what you intend to do about wrongs that you have committed.

Another thing that can be done to help your stepchild over the hurts which a divorce brings is to have another person talk to him—someone whom the child accepts and respects. If this person is objective and trustworthy in the eyes of your child, there can be some positive help for the child in talking his problems out and sharing his feelings with someone other than his parents.

One helpful thing that some stepparents have found useful in dealing with their children is that of asking key questions that penetrate quickly to their innermost feelings. For example: "What do you believe I could have done to prevent the divorce?"

Or, "What do you think God wants me to do now that all this has happened?" Or, "What do you miss the most about your mother?" Or, "What do you really feel about your stepdad?"

If you decide to use these questions with your child, take a couple of things into consideration before you do. For one thing, don't prejudge your child or even anticipate your child's answers. Be willing to let him share what he really feels without threats from you. Secondly, relate carefully to the age of your child. A child in elementary school will respond much differently than a child in junior high (tough period) or high school.

What Are the Basic Needs of Your Stepchildren?

When a divorce and remarriage occur, certain basic needs of the stepchildren must be dealt with or further problems will come. As we have already pointed out, the real trouble in handling a child who is not your own did not begin with your remarriage, but with the first day that the child learned of the divorce. Divorce can shatter the emotional security and perspective of the child. The basic question is "Why me?" The child becomes confused, bitter, hurt, and angry. He or she begins to ask, "What have I done to deserve this? I must be pretty awful for this to happen to me!"

One of my pastor friends, who works with children's ministries, has done some research on the basic needs of children who have been devastated by divorce. Based on the things which remarried parents told him, he came up with the following eight needs of children who have experienced divorce. He says, "These eight needs must be met in order for the child to survive divorce in his home."

1. *The need to accept the situation as it is.*

The child will fight this, of course. The child will often use rebellion to force the parents to reconsider. Many children are unwilling to acknowledge God's sovereignty in divorce. Romans 8:28 says, "And we know that God causes all things to work together for good to those who love God, to those who are called according to His purpose." But, try to tell that to your child at the time of divorce! Not only is there a lack of understanding because of age or emotional hurt, but there is also the confusion in a child's mind between what God may have allowed to happen and what his parents have done to destroy his home.

It is not God who causes divorce; it is caused by people who are unwilling to obey what God's Word says about their commitment to one another in marriage. The child must understand that God's plan is violated when divorce occurs, and he must be willing to trust God to bring some good into his life through the experience. Depending on the age of your child, that's not easy to understand.

I tried to tell a ten-year-old girl whose parents had gotten a divorce that God would bring some good out of this in the future, and she replied: "Why is God punishing me?" I reassured this little girl that God was not punishing her and I tried to explain that God loves her no matter what has happened. I told her that one day she would understand much more about why it happened than she did right then. But, to tell you the truth, my words seemed pretty empty next to the heartache this little girl was experiencing. It took her quite a while (over six months) before she even wanted to talk about it again. When I see things like that, it makes me hate divorce. No wonder God hates it.

2. *The need to rebuild trust in God and ultimately in people.*

One of the first things that happens to the child whose parents have divorced is a loss of confidence. If they can't trust their parents, who can they trust? When children ask, "Why me?" they are really asking God. The child is calling God's faithfulness to him into question. He is no longer willing to trust God with the responsibility of directing his life.

At this point, we must remind the child that nothing, not even death itself, can separate him from the love of God (Romans 8:38, 39). God operates in a different way than we do, and His plans can change ours at any moment He believes it is necessary in order to accomplish His purposes. God is not untrustworthy; He simply thinks and acts differently than we do with our limited perspective (Isaiah 55:8, 9). Once the child has learned to trust God again, he will learn to trust other people, because ultimately God is in control of those people. Even those in authority over us were placed there by God (Romans 13:1). Trust is essential for obedience to God and to one's parents.

One sixteen-year-old girl shared with me that she lost confidence in her father because he divorced her mother and married another woman. She became bitter over this situation for several reasons. On one occasion when she knew that her father was seeing this other woman, her father assured her that he would not divorce his wife, and would get his life straightened out. When that didn't happen, the daughter felt that her dad could not be trusted to keep his word. She then began to lose confidence in the Lord and His promises. She also felt that she was to blame for this situation. On many occasions, her mother and father would argue over how to deal with her. After the divorce, she thought much about all the trouble she had caused her parents (especially during her junior high years), and felt that her rebellion contributed to her dad leaving the home for another woman. I told her that such was not the case. He left because he got involved with another woman contrary to the clear teaching of God's Word. I told her that we are all sinners and we are all (including herself!) capable of terrible sins. We talked about God's love and forgiveness and what can be learned through such a tragic set of circumstances. I reminded her that her dad still loved her, and that his sin was not caused by her earlier rebellion. We both made a pledge to pray for him.

This story has a happy ending for that girl. She not only began to trust God once again, but her confidence in others was restored and she began to grow spiritually in a marvelous way. Today she is looking forward to marriage, and planning to serve the Lord some day on the mission field.

3. *The need to forgive those who have shattered his world.*

In addition to accepting the situation as it is and rebuilding trust in God and others, the child whose parents have divorced must also learn to forgive his parents.

The needs to forgive and to be forgiven are probably two of the greatest needs any human being experiences. A child of divorce may have very strong feelings about his home. These feelings may be manifested in anger and an unwillingness to forgive the offending parent, or parents. The child must be made to understand God's perspective of forgiveness, which is to forgive unconditionally. The grace which God has extended to us by forgiving us is the pattern which God would have us to follow when someone sins against us. In Matthew 6:14, 15, Jesus says that if we don't forgive others, God will not forgive us. Without such forgiveness, there can be no true restoration in the home. The home will be a place of tension and isolation rather than love, warmth, and good communication. Without forgiveness, any hope of peace and calm in the home is severely limited.

One of our pastors related to me how difficult it was for the son of one of our single parents in the church to forgive his father, who had left the home for another woman. This boy's anger toward other men was rooted in his anger toward his father. Whenever a man in the church tried to give this boy counsel or advice, he would become hostile and tell him to "get lost."

That boy needed to forgive his dad, but it did not come easily. In one of our Sunday School classes, the lesson was on the death of Christ and the suffering which He experienced in our behalf. The boy's anger subsided and his desire to forgive his father became an immediate goal as the teacher of that class talked about what happened to Jesus Christ and how He had forgiven those who had persecuted Him. A wonderful encounter happened later that week as the boy called his dad and sought his forgiveness. The dad was deeply moved and apologized to his son, reassuring him of his love for him, and asking his boy to pray for him. The attitude of that boy immediately changed. He has become a blessing to his mother instead of a burden.

4. *The need for someone to talk to about the divorce.*

I shared the importance of this point earlier, but it needs to be reemphasized. This is one of the basic needs of a child of divorce. The parent who has custody, or both parents if they share custody of the child, may not be objective. The parents may be working through their own emotions and thus are unable to listen well or counsel effectively. The child really needs two things: a person to share his real feelings with and someone to help him deal with those feelings.

We have two responsibilities in relationship to this need. First, we can remind the child that God always has a listening ear. We can cast all of our anxiety (worry) on God, because He cares for us (1 Peter 5:7). That's a promise we can all claim. Secondly, we can try to be a friend who "sticks closer than a brother" (Proverbs 18:24). It is impossible for most children to approach a problem objectively without assistance from someone who has an objective perspective. We can be that someone who can help these children put their world back together. But, we will have to take the time to do so. Does the child know that he or she can call on you at any time for help? Are you there when the child needs someone to talk to?

5. *The need to learn how to relate to others.*

This is one of the most difficult areas for a child of divorce to handle. A child who lives in a family that has experienced a divorce is now "different" from other children. He may feel self-conscious, withdrawn, or simply out of place. He may have to deal with questions like, "Is your dad coming to the game?" Or, "Why haven't I seen your mom lately?" Or, maybe even this one, "I saw your dad with another woman the other day!"

These questions and remarks cut deeply into the emotions of these sensitive children and can cause a great deal of harm if not dealt with properly. We can help by talking through these questions with the child and relieving any guilt the child may have as a result of the parent's leaving. Once the child feels good about himself, we can help him think through some good replies to these embarrassing questions.

Remind the child not to be angry, but to respond gently to his friends because this is what the Lord would have him do (Proverbs 15:1). We should help the child learn to turn these comments around and use them to encourage other children to be thankful for their own parents.

One of our single parents, whose wife left him for another man, shared this beautiful incident with me. His son was asked by his friends at school, "Did your mom divorce your dad?" The boy responded, "It's none of your business!" These friends then started to get on him about it. He became angry and did not handle it well. Later that day when he got home from school, he told his dad about it. His dad then patiently helped his boy with this problem by going over possible answers. The next day at school, one of his buddies came up and said, "Hey, what's this I hear about your mom?" He replied, "Thanks for asking. I sure hope you will join me and my dad in prayer for my mom. She's a great lady, and I love her, but right now she's going through a tough time. Please pray with me, will you?" His friend was amazed and said, "Sure!" The boy's answer was uncharacteristic of teenagers who have experienced a divorce in their home. But thanks to an understanding father's help, he was able to respond well to the question, and it made him feel great.

6. *The need to learn to function in the new environment.*

Many children of divorce become what we call "latchkey kids." These are children who wear a door key on a chain around their neck. When they get home from school, their mom or dad (or both) is still at work and the house is empty. A child in this situation is more inclined to be lonely or afraid and will have more opportunity to get into trouble.

This is a sensitive issue and must be approached carefully. We must not communicate to the child that we mistrust him, but instead we should tell him that this is an opportunity for him to demonstrate that he is a responsible person. Give him certain responsibilities that must be fulfilled before the parent arrives home. Suggest that this would be a good time to do homework or personal Bible study. Most of all, the parents should always leave a note or something to remind the child of his presence in the home and his soon return. It will be difficult for the child to adjust, but we know that he can surely do it through Christ who strengthens him (Philippians 4:13).

The best answer to this situation is for one of the parents to be at home when the children come home. When a child has experienced the divorce of his parents, a certain insecurity is there already. If the remarriage of one of the child's parents has put him into a new home and new environment, there will still be a certain amount of insecurity. A parent at home when the child is home will help the child to overcome fear and anxiety caused by the difficult changes in his family structure.

The child needs time to adjust. Parents who try to force the child to respond to the new environment before the child has had a chance to adapt emotionally and psychologically will find strong resistance by the child. Further problems of resentment and rebellion can be created if the child is not given some time to work things through and learn about his new environment.

The child will need to know the limitations and restrictions of his new environment. He will probably test the parents on this point. The child needs to know the guidelines. The trust and confidence of the child can be rebuilt if the child sees the parents following through on what guidelines and rules there are. A certain amount of discipline and authority is essential for developing the security of the child.

One of the remarried couples in our church was greatly concerned because their child was usually not at home when they returned from work. What they had failed to understand was the way the child felt when he came home from school. His mother worked all during the time of her divorce, and the child was on his own after school for about two years. Now that she had remarried, she continued to work when she really didn't have to do so, for her new husband made enough money to care for the family. I challenged her to consider quitting her job so that she could be home when her son returned from school. At least she could look for employment that would allow her to be home when the boy was there. She discussed it with her husband and found out that he felt the same. So, she quit her job, and after just a few months, their son's attitude had completely changed.

The above story may not repeat itself in every situation, but in my opinion, one of the parents needs to be home when children come home from school. It is dangerous to the emotional health of the child to come home to an empty house—especially after a divorce. It frightens the child and causes him to think that one of these days one or both of his parents will not come home.

7. *The need to be responsible for his own actions.*

When a child suddenly finds himself in a world of unfamiliar emotions and circumstances, he often will rebel and use the divorce or the remarriage as an excuse for his disobedience. The single parent may also use the circumstances in the home to excuse the misbehavior of the children. Remarried couples will often find the same kind of response and not know how to handle it.

Children must be taught to assume responsibility for their own actions. We are all accountable to God for what we do and say, not the conduct of others. The Bible clearly says that we will be both rewarded and punished according to our personal behavior (Romans 14:10–12; 2 Corinthians 5:10; Revelation 20:11–15).

God does not excuse our behavior and we should not excuse the behavior of others. We are not told to excuse or ignore, but to forgive. There is a big difference between those two things!

I did not enjoy talking with a twelve-year-old girl about her attitude of rebellion toward her parents. She was clearly using her dad's past divorce and his marriage to her stepmom as an excuse for her rebellion. When I confronted her about it, she got mad. She finally blurted out, "My dad deserves what he's getting after what he did to me!" Now I had the answer I was looking for. This girl was punishing her father for divorcing her mother and marrying this other woman. When I told her that God would hold her accountable for what she was doing, she began to cry. She said, "But that isn't fair!" I said, "It's not fair for you to play God and try to hurt your dad, either!" She said, "I love my dad!" I responded, "Then why don't you show it!" After a few more minutes, she seemed to understand more of what she was doing to her father. After our talk, she went home and apologized to her parents, but admitted why she was doing it. They responded in a beautiful way, telling her that they understood and were sorry for all that had happened. They all realized that they had to start over again, trusting God to rebuild their relationships. Things are now much better in that home.

8. *The need to be loved.*

No doubt you have been wondering when we were going to mention this tremendous need of every child. We all want to be loved and children of divorce and remarriage are no exception. A recent publication for parents said that the average person needs about twenty hugs a day just to get by. It went on to say that hugging is one way to show your love for someone, and especially children. Even though you say you love your child, he may not feel loved, so it is essential that you demonstrate your love for him.

A child of divorce and remarriage is very vulnerable, and many of these children think that when a parent leaves the home, he or she no longer loves the children. The single parent must continually show his or her love for the children. It is especially a difficult time for the children as well as that parent. When remarriage occurs, the need is still there and is sometimes intensified. The child wonders whether the new parent loves him more than the parent who left.

Henry Bliss was really struggling with his stepson. He loved his new wife, Mary, very much, and it was their decision to keep Mary's boy. Henry had no children of his own. He asked me, "Pastor, I try to love that boy, but he just doesn't like me." I said, "Do you hug him much?" He said, "I've never been much for that." I said, "Well, you'd better change!" I went on to tell Henry how much his stepson needed a show of physical affection from him. Henry was uneasy, but he went home and tried. He called me in a couple of days and said, "Pastor, I just can't thank you enough for our little talk the other day. My stepson has responded to me in a great way since I started giving him a big hug every morning and every night." I said, "Keep it up, Henry, keep it up!"

The day the children hear that one of their parents is leaving is devastating to them. It often takes years for them to recover. The hurt is deep and carries over into relationships with stepparents. The real needs of the children must be dealt with on a daily basis. Many remarried couples have testified to the terrible home situations that have been created by rebellious stepchildren. You can't run away from these problems. If the stepchildren are in your home, they need your love and attention. It takes God's grace and strength to deal with children who are not your own but are now living with you in your home.

Parents must learn to seek wisdom from God's Word. We need to spend time in prayer, seeking God's help. It is not easy, but God's power and love can meet every situation we face. There needs to be open communication between stepparents and stepchildren; they need to face their inability to cope with situations and be willing to work for peace and harmony in the home by committing themselves to God and His Word for direction and guidance.

Questions for Reflection

1. What is the real trouble most remarried couples face?
2. When does the real trouble begin?
3. What are the basic needs of your children?
4. What needs do you see right now in your own family because of what you have read?
5. What things can you change or do that would help your family situation?

4

The Legal Hassles

I had never thought much about this problem. But one day a friend of mine who has divorced and remarried showed me something that opened my eyes. He had a briefcase full of papers regarding his divorce and the custody of his children and his wife's children. This man's former partner and his wife's former husband have been driving him and his wife crazy with this "stuff." When I see this couple in church every week, I see a happy, vibrant loving man and woman who readily serve the Lord in every way possible. Little did I realize the tremendous struggles that were going on in their lives because of divorce and remarriage.

Remarried couples have spoken about these "legal hassles" as "constant irritations," and have made statements to me like, "It's enough to drive you crazy!" One wife said, "My former husband is doing this deliberately to me! He is trying to get even!" Another husband told me, "My former wife will not leave us alone! I've talked to my attorney about it on many occasions."

Arguments, confrontations, lies, deception, manipulation, theft, cheating, shouting, swearing, physical abuse, harassment—you name it—it often comes with divorce and remarriage! The bitterness and resentment can remain for years. Remarried couples have to live with it as a part of their lives, and their children are deeply affected by it, often not knowing whom to believe or what to think about all of these "hassles."

In the book, *The Divorce Handbook,* by James T. Friedman (published by Random House), the author gives reasons why you may need to read his book. Reading over his list, I could not help realizing that these reasons touch upon only half of the problems which many divorced and remarried couples are experiencing. He says a person needs legal help in the following situations:

1. You don't want a divorce but your spouse just filed for one or has mentioned the possibility.
2. You have just come from your first appointment with a lawyer and he used a number of words you didn't understand but didn't ask him to explain.
3. Your spouse is jeopardizing your job with phone calls to your employer and/or lies to your friends and coworkers.
4. Your spouse has missed his temporary support payment for the tenth time.
5. Every time you call your lawyer you forget two points of the five you wanted to cover, because he sounds in a hurry.
6. Your divorce seems to be standing still, and you're standing in quicksand.
7. With inflation you're bleeding from support payments. Can they be modified?
8. Court continuances are ruining your schedule. Doesn't anybody else work?

9. Your lawyer is in court or in conference every time you call.
10. You never know when you'll see your children. They seem brainwashed against you.
11. The silver and the piano are missing.
12. You have agreed to too large a support payment, and can't manage financially.
13. You feel helpless and your life seems out of control.

Let's face it—these situations are only a small fraction of what divorced and remarried people must face. One of my remarried friends supports two families, two businesses, two houses, and along with it all, must endure a hypochondriac former spouse who hassles him about every little thing. His present wife can't take it, and so he does his best to keep all of these things from her. He's frustrated and wonders about the whole thing from time to time in a way that makes me think he's contemplating a permanent vacation to the island of Tahiti!

Whether we like it or not, the problems of divorce, remarriage, child custody and support, and property rights demand some legal and financial counsel. The laws of each state are different and often quite complex. They change frequently and require legal interpretation. It is important for you to keep your records and documents in a safe place, and no matter how long it's been since your divorce and/or remarriage, don't throw away the papers that deal with these matters. It is well known that issues can come up years later with the changing emotional responses of former spouses, especially toward their children.

The legal hassles which you endure will not be the same as someone else's. It is always wise to avoid the advice of friends and seek correct information from legal counsel. Know what you are doing before you do it.

What Are the Major Legal Issues to Be Faced?

While each person's case is different, certain common issues must be faced by each person who experiences divorce and re-marriage.

1. *The divorce itself.*

It is a devastating experience in and of itself, but often the problems that come later can be just as troublesome. I am con-tinually amazed in my pastoral ministry at the many ramifica-tions of a divorce and how they can continue to hassle a person long after a divorce is supposedly settled. At the time of the di-vorce, certain problems need to be resolved. One very serious one deals with your relationship with your former spouse. We have talked about many things already in this regard, but let's look at a few more.

Divorce tends to bring out the worst in people. People do crazy things that they later regret. Half of what is said to you by your partner from whom you are divorcing cannot be trusted. People going through a divorce try to deceive and manipulate their spouses. Above all, you should not get into arguments with your spouse or agree to sign anything without first talking to your law-yer or a Christian arbitrator from your church.

Harassment by your spouse is quite common. If it did not happen to you, you are one of the fortunate ones. A great deal of argument usually takes place over the children and such things as property, furniture, and cars. Sometimes there is physical abuse or violence. There are laws against such abuse, and you should not tolerate it under any circumstances.

Sometimes a spouse will leave the house in order to get away from the place of conflict and turmoil, but will later regret that decision. A physical separation may affect the decision in later divorce proceedings. If a wife or husband seeks the custody of the children, but left the house at some point before the divorce, she or he will be at a disadvantage when the actual custody proceedings begin. Also, the longer you are gone, the more difficult it will be to reenter the house if your spouse is resisting you. Serious legal questions can develop in relation to this. Seek counsel before you make such a decision.

Dating during the time of your separation can often be treated as moral misconduct and may affect some of the issues of your future remarriage or divorce settlements, and may especially affect the child custody issue.

Do not be surprised to find a former spouse trying to change the decisions of your divorce or child custody proceedings. This is one of those sad "legal hassles" that comes to remarried couples. When these things come up, don't panic or worry about possible loss or further turmoil to your new family relationships. Commit these matters to the Lord, and trust Him to give you His peace (Philippians 4:6, 7) and the ability to deal with these matters (2 Timothy 1:7) without fear or revenge.

2. *Child custody.*

No grief is as great as this problem. Divorced spouses often fight over their children without regard for the children's feelings. The children almost always suffer during these experiences, because they are torn between the two fighting parents, and must now face divided loyalties.

The child should be invited to say what he or she really feels about the situation when a divorce is imminent. Don't suppress those feelings in the child. They need to be expressed. Discuss with him what is going to take place and that a decision must be reached as to where the child is going to live—with the mother or the father, or in some cases, with another relative.

The sad truth is that many couples do not handle this matter very well. Lawyers tell us that some of the worst kinds of court battles result from fights over the custody of the children. The court will be concerned with which parent has been principally responsible for the care of the child as well as the competence of that parent in the future. Sometimes the children will be asked to testify, though this is usually not a good idea. It is very hard on a child to testify against one of his parents.

Joint custody is not often recommended by marriage counselors or psychologists, but it is often used to acknowledge the fitness of both parents in caring for their children. It usually leads to enormous problems in practical application. Split custody puts the children with one parent part of the year, and with the other parent the other part. Each parent has authority over the child during the time the child is with him/her. In most cases, it is confusing to the child, and the child has difficulty adjusting to this arrangement.

Temporary custody is usually given to the parent who is still residing in the home where the child is living at the time of the divorce proceedings. This type of custody continues to leave matters "up-in-the-air," and should not be continued for very long. We always advise remarried couples to settle all issues as permanently as possible.

One of the great tragedies that some remarried couples have had to face is the kidnapping of one of the children by a former spouse. Usually, the former spouse takes the child out of state. In 1981, the federal Parental Kidnapping Prevention Act was passed, requiring all state courts to follow the Uniform Child Custody Jurisdiction Act. This act determines which state has jurisdiction to decide a custody dispute and how the matter is going to be resolved.

One of the remarried couples of our church experienced just such a "kidnapping." They had been married for many years, and had been raising one of the wife's children by a previous marriage. One day, her former husband went by the elementary school where his son was in attendance and snatched him from the playground. For two years, this couple had no idea what had happened to this son. Eventually, he was found and returned. It was a very sad and traumatic experience which neither they nor I will forget—a sad reminder of the many "legal hassles" which come to remarried couples.

3. *Child support.*

Child support is another "legal hassle" that plagues the divorced and remarried couples. It is different from child custody. The amount of child support is based on the income and assets of the parents. When a spouse remarries, it is important to know that the new spouse has no obligation to support someone else's children. However, if the new spouse is caring for most of the expenses of the child, that will affect the amount of support that a former spouse may be required to contribute. But courts will not increase or decrease child support based solely on the income of the new spouse.

One of our members, who has been divorced and remarried, pays child support to his former wife to care for his son. Through a set of unbelievable circumstances and pressures, his former wife refused to allow him to visit his son anymore. He thought that the way to handle this was to cut off the child support. He was surprised to learn that he must pay support even if visitation is not allowed.

4. *Visitation rights.*

I grow weary of hearing about this problem, but it is a hard reality in the lives of stepparents and stepchildren, as well as natural parents and children. One cannot appreciate the desire of a former spouse to visit his or her children until he has been in that position. One father said, "Dave, I can't wait until the next weekend when I can see my little girl again! I miss her so very much. I love her more than I can tell you, and I feel terrible about what has happened!" This father experienced divorce from a wife who was having an affair with another man; through her clever manipulation, she was able to take custody of their girl. The former wife knew how much he loved that girl, and she punishes him every time he comes to visit his daughter. She makes it difficult for him, the time is always changed, and there's always some problem. He gets so weary of it, but he would not miss seeing his little girl every other weekend.

Visitation rights vary. Sometimes they are granted for only once a month or twice a month (usually weekends), with alternate national holidays. An extended period of "visitation" may be given during the summer. Sometimes, the parent with whom the child is living doesn't really care about the child and is glad to have the former spouse pick up the child and do some "babysitting" whenever the former spouse wants. Every situation is different.

Be Prepared for the Questions!

When these legal hassles come, you had better be prepared for the interrogation by the lawyers. They will ask all kinds of personal and difficult questions that will often determine the outcome of these cases. Their questions may involve possible physical abuse, mental cruelty, adultery suspicions and accusations, child neglect and abuse, income and property rights, discipline of the children, and financial habits. Many people are shocked to discover the ends to which a former spouse will go to have a decision rendered in his or her favor.

The Bible exhorts us to be truthful at all times, and not to seek revenge. One of the most helpful passages to read before entering into any of these "legal hassles" is Romans 12:17–21:

> Never pay back evil for evil to anyone. Respect what is right in the sight of all men. If possible, so far as it depends on you, be at peace with all men. Never take your own revenge, beloved, but leave room for the wrath of God, for it is written, "Vengeance is Mine, I will

repay, says the Lord." But if your enemy is hungry, feed him, and if he is thirsty, give him a drink; for in so doing you will heap burning coals upon his head. Do not be overcome by evil, but overcome evil with good.

Several years ago a man who was going through all of these "legal hassles" with his ex-wife came to see me. They had fights over property, money, children, and other matters. He was insisting on his "rights" but he was not happy about it. As a result, he was losing weight, feeling irritable most of the time, doing poorly at his job, and generally being hard to get along with. His spirit was captured by revenge. I said to him, "Dick, why don't you give it up?" He said, "What do you mean by that?" I said, "You are ruining your life by trying to get back at your wife for what she did to you. Why don't you stop and begin trusting God more?" He was a little upset with me that day, but it started to work on him. He was living for one thing: to get even. The trouble is, it never happens.

Dick had not remarried and neither had his wife. The children lived with her. I challenged him to change his whole attitude and to let her have what she wanted. He said, "She'll really take advantage of that!" I said, "Let her!" He agreed, and we both prayed that God would give him a sweet and loving spirit, and that he would have the attitude of Job, who said, "The Lord gave and the Lord has taken away. Blessed be the name of the Lord" (Job 1:21).

Much to his surprise, his new attitude and spirit began to change the heart of his wife. She could not believe it. She began to ask questions of others about her husband. Before too long, they were seeing each other again socially, and after about two years, she was convinced—he had changed. I had the joy of remarrying them.

I may not have touched on all the "legal hassles" you have had through your divorce and/or remarriage, but I do not believe it is wise to seek revenge—ever! You are only hurting yourself, not only at the present time, but more importantly, for the future. Don't let it happen to you. If you don't love your former spouse, at least be polite and courteous. Don't try to get even. Don't poison the minds of your children toward your former spouse. It will eventually come back to hurt you. Maintain a sweet Christlike spirit at all times and learn to take your burdens to the Lord and leave them there.

Questions for Reflection

1. What kind of "legal hassles" have you had and what have you done about them?
2. What are the four major legal issues that most couples must face?
3. What kind of attitude is best in dealing with your former spouse?

5

The Financial Agreement

Bob and his wife, Peggy, had been married before, and brought some financial problems into their present marriage. After Peggy's former husband left her, she had to get a job to support herself and her two children. God was good to her, and she began to prosper financially. She not only paid off all her debts, but began to invest her money wisely and within a few years she was independently wealthy. She owned her home, car, and many beautiful antiques. She had set up a trust fund for each of her children.

When Bob was divorced from his first wife, he had many debts, and also was required by the court to provide support for his two children who were given to his wife. He had some difficult financial pressures when he met Peggy. After a few short months of dating, they decided to get married. They never thought much about what problems they would face in terms of financial pressures, but only a few weeks after they were married, some problems began to surface. They argued a great deal over these matters. Bob wanted to consolidate everything that he and Peggy had brought into the marriage. His debts became "their problems" and her wealth and assets would become "his" by marriage. Peggy was resentful of this arrangement. Why should she have to help pay the debts of his previous marriage? She felt insecure after her first husband's departure. What if Bob would take off some day with another woman? Peggy insisted on keeping a separate bank account, and that "her things" should be kept in her name only. Bob was furious. The marriage almost ended over these matters. Fortunately, they both sought counsel and were able to resolve their disagreements.

Their story could be repeated many times. Though the details might change, and the financial obligations might be different, most remarried couples have had to face these problems. How you work them out may affect the success of your marriage more than you realize.

Ed Jones and his wife faced a similar problem. Ed's wife obtained a beautiful home when her divorce was settled. Ed's former wife left him for another man, and wanted nothing from Ed. He had a house, two cars, and a successful business. The problem was, which house would they live in, and what would they do with the other house? They both felt insecure in dealing with the problem, but they were wise enough to settle this matter *before* they got married. They handled it in the presence of a marriage counselor and it worked out to the satisfaction of them both. Ed wanted his prospective wife to live in the home she wanted to have. She chose her own house. Ed then sold his house and put all the assets into a new joint bank account. Ed's wife had a car she was making payments on, and Ed had two cars. Once again, he asked her which of the three cars she would like to have. She again wanted her own car. Ed then paid off the debt of that car, and sold one of his cars. They seem very happy in their remarriage.

Couples cannot ignore the financial problems they will inherit in a new marriage. They are in a different position than those marrying for the first time. It is not enough to say, "Don't worry, we'll work these problems out in time!" Our interviews with remarried couples have brought out one special need—these financial matters must be settled *before* the marriage takes place.

Important Financial Information

Before you remarry, you need to know some facts about the financial situation of your partner. If you have already remarried, and you do not know these facts, you'd better find out as soon as possible. The following facts are important for both partners to know and understand.

1. *The income of your partner.*

Is it sufficient to cover the debts both of you have? If both partners have jobs, is the income of both partners to be put together in one common account? Can you support the new family on your present income?

2. *The debts of your partner.*

These debts may include mortgage payments on a house, car loans, child support, alimony, and credit cards. Make sure that your marital partner knows your financial obligations.

3. *Insurance policies of your partner.*

These policies include life insurance, health insurance, homeowner's policies, and others. Are the children included? What about the stepchildren?

4. *The assets of your partner.*

What does your partner own? Is there a house, car, furniture, or bank account that you do not know about? Will these assets remain in your partner's name, or will they be held jointly? Do any of these belong in whole or in part to a former partner?

5. *The spending habits of your partner.*

Have you seen your partner's checking account? Do you know how your partner spends money? Does your partner keep a budget? Is your partner "tight" with his or her money? Does your partner give regularly to the church and charitable organizations? Are there any hobbies or activities which seemingly cost a great deal of money? How much is spent by your partner on entertainment, dining out, recreation, vacations, clothes?

All of these questions are vital to establishing harmony and unity in your new marriage. Foresight is better than hindsight in this case. People contemplating a remarriage should enter that new relationship with their eyes wide open when it comes to financial matters.

General Principles for Financial Unity

Thanks to the advice and comments of many remarried couples, we can list some general principles that all couples can follow in order to achieve oneness in financial matters.

1. *Be completely honest and open about your finances.*

One husband we interviewed said, "My mistake was not telling my new wife about a previous financial arrangement I had with my first wife. I didn't want to bother her with it. Besides, I didn't think she would understand." He was right on one point—when she found out about it, she didn't understand. She became very insecure and felt threatened by it.

Most couples who were interviewed warned about keeping things from the new partner. Everything should be "out in the open." The chances for marital disharmony increase when you are not honest or open about your financial situation.

When a friend told us about her "secret bank account" that her husband did not know existed, I responded, "If I were you, I would tell your husband immediately. If he finds out, he will think that he cannot trust you." These "secret" financial arrangements are damaging to the marital relationship and may cause your partner to have suspicions and doubts as to your loyalty and dependability.

2. *Put all assets under both names.*

Many times during the interviews with remarried couples this point would be emphasized. One of the first acts of the new couple should be to have all documents changed to read "Mr._____ and Mrs._____." It is important to do this together and to make it an official ceremony, sealing your commitment to one another. Change your wills accordingly and be sure to include the stepchildren in your care.

It is sad how many remarried couples have not yet done this. Some of the reasons given for not doing it are most enlightening. A wife said, "I couldn't trust my first husband, so how can I trust my husband now?" One husband told me, "Before I do that, I want to make sure my wife really loves me." One wife shared this information: "My parents gave me that car, and it was before my remarriage. It belongs to me, and I don't see why I should put my husband's name on the title." One wife cried when discussing her separate bank account and investments, saying, "I've been married twice before, and both former husbands ran off with other women. I'm not taking any chances this time." One man told me, "My house belonged to my father and grandfather, and I have left it in my will to my son. Why should I put my new wife's name on it? I'll take care of her in another way."

The list could go on and on. Regardless of how valid the reasons may seem, marital unity is affected by our financial decisions. They often say more than our words.

The primary reason for the reluctance of the remarried to put all assets into the names of both partners seems to be insecurity. There is a fear that the other partner will do what the former partner may have done. Self-protection is a strong, natural trait of us all. To give up our independence and put our complete trust in another person is not easy.

The great danger of keeping assets and accounts separate from each other is that of an independent spirit. First Corinthians 11:11 teaches the interdependency of husband and wife. I asked one 42-year-old husband how he felt about his new wife's decision to keep her own bank account and assets in her own name, and not his, and he said, "It makes me feel like she doesn't need me or trust me."

3. *Depend on the husband's salary for all basic living costs.*

The man has been instructed by God (1 Timothy 5:8) to be the provider of the family. His emotional and psychological structure demands that his family depend upon him for basic needs. When people marry for the second time, there needs to be a return to this basic principle. During the days after divorce, the wife usually learns to be independent and to provide for herself and her children without a husband's help. When she remarries, she must learn all over again how to depend upon her husband. She must need his protection and provision as much as he needs her to depend upon him. Most remarried couples have experienced some adjustment problems in this regard.

One couple with whom I talked were having some difficulties adjusting to each other's life-style and needs. They both had good salaries and great talent. When I suggested that the husband's salary be the one they lived on, the wife said, "What do I do with the money I make?" I suggested that they put it into a special account for things like furniture or appliances, or make it a vacation account. The husband was really responsive to this, because his number one concern was that she did not really need him or depend upon him. She was already financially independent.

About three months later, they shared with me how well their marriage was going now. They did what I suggested, and a new relationship developed between them. The wife was once again depending upon a husband's leadership and provision. His smiles told me how happy he was for the change.

4. *Treat all children equally.*

This particular problem was brought up frequently by remarried couples who participated in the interviews. Whether we admit it or not, we tend to favor our own children over our stepchildren. This is often seen in financial matters. One child receives a greater allowance than another child without a justifiable reason. One child receives more presents than another child. The rivalry between the children can be more serious when these conditions exist.

It is quite common for parents to reward their own children in a greater way than their stepchildren when they make out their wills. When this happens, it simply reveals that the new family created in the remarriage has not been completely bound together as one. If you want your stepchildren to feel fully accepted, then treat them financially as you would your own children.

When one father challenged me on this point of equal support for his stepchildren, I said, "If you don't do this, why are you taking them on as your children?" His answer was quite revealing. He said, "I have to. She won't marry me unless I do." His problem was that he wanted a new wife, but not her children. Until he gets a father's heart for those children he has no business marrying their mother.

5. *Require mutual agreement on all future financial agreements and expenditures.*

Husband and wife should discuss all financial matters

thoroughly, and mutually agree on all expenditures. A common practice among the remarried is for one of the partners to incur a debt or make a major purchase without discussing it with the other partner. Sometimes this is caused by the independent spirit that developed between the time of the divorce and the remarriage. It is not done intentionally. You reason that you have a perfect right to do it because you are using "*your* money."

The problem here is that you forget all assets are now "joint" and do not just belong to you. The more you seek your partner's advice and counsel on financial decisions, the greater will be the intimacy and closeness of your relationship.

One remarried woman told us that her husband really got angry, and then hurt, because she went out one day and bought new furniture for their living room without asking him about it. She said, "But it was my money that I spent. I thought he would be happy about it. Besides, it was on sale!" She did not realize that it hurt her husband, not because of the money, but because she didn't ask his opinion. Her decision emphasized her independence, not their marital unity.

The problems of remarriage are unique, and this is obvious when you face financial matters. You must forget the past and commit yourself totally to your new relationship. If you can't do that, it is better that you not remarry until you are able to make such a commitment. Remarriage is starting all over again. In order to do it right, the old attachments and agreements must be broken, and new ones established. Every remarried couple must be sure that there are "no strings attached" and "no loopholes" to their commitment. Take the words "what if" out of your vocabulary. Have no "plan B" in case your "plan A" doesn't work. Burn all your bridges and do all you can to build the unity and interdependency of your new marriage relationship. With the Lord's help, you can do it.

Questions for Reflection

1. What kind of financial information about your partner should you have?
2. What general principles should guide remarried couples in financial matters?
3. What can you do with your financial situation to emphasize your "oneness" with your partner?
4. What needs to be changed in your life after reading this chapter? Will you discuss it with your partner?
5. What would you do over again if you had the chance?
6. Is everything you have in your partner's name also?

6

The Sexual Adjustments

My interviews of remarried couples revealed a wide diversity of attitudes and practices regarding sex. It was difficult to discern any common denominator among the various people interviewed. Some couples were well adjusted and expressed great joy and satisfaction in their sexual relationship. Many couples were having serious problems of adjustment, and several of them did not know why. Some spoke of the difficulty of giving themselves completely to another person when their former partner had hurt them so in the past. Several couples were disappointed in their sexual life in remarriage. It was not what they had expected it to be.

One wife put it this way: "I find it difficult to relate sexually to my husband when I remember what my former husband said and did. I've lost a lot of confidence, and feel many times that I'm unable to satisfy a man's sexual desires. My former husband made me think that, and it's hard not to be controlled by those former experiences."

A discouraged husband said, "I'm afraid to tell my new wife what I really like in terms of sex, because she's always wondering how it was with my first wife and whether the sex we have now is better or not."

One husband whose first wife rarely had sex with him, and whose second wife is quite aggressive, remarked: "I have no complaints! It's great now!"

Another husband told me: "Sex now is a duty. Very little passion is involved. We stick to the 'missionary position'!"

One of the best comments came from a wife whose former husband ran off with another woman. Her present husband has been great to her: "My sex life is very rewarding now because I can fully trust the man I am married to. He's committed to me, and believe me, I know the difference!"

Talking with the remarried about sex is quite different from discussing sex with those planning to get married for the first time. The "joy of discovery" is missing, and the hurts of the former relationships have left their scars. Those who have been through the pain of divorce and the challenge of remarriage seem much more open to talk about their problems and much more willing to receive any help that is offered. Their past has taught them much about failure and deceit. They have learned that what goes on in bed is not always a real evaluation of a marriage. They have also learned that true romance and deep love for another person cannot be developed by a moment's encounter in bed.

One of the tragedies of today's culture is the toleration of sexual involvements outside of marriage. Most of the individuals interviewed had experienced sex after their divorces, and some of them felt obligated to marry the person with whom they had sexual relations. These sexual involvements have definitely affected their ability to enjoy sex and feel satisfied. Almost all of the couples said that they wished they had never had any sex outside of marriage. This viewpoint only reconfirmed in my mind the importance of the Bible's teaching about sex. Sex with one person "until death do us part" is still the best way. The Bible condemns any sexual relations outside of marriage, and exalts the relationship of husband and wife. Hebrews 13:4 says:

Let marriage be held in honor among all, and let the marriage bed be undefiled; for fornicators and adulterers God will judge.

How Do You Deal with Thoughts of Your Former Spouse?

Many people spoke of this problem. In one sense, it is to be expected. If you spend many years with a man or woman, it will be very difficult to wipe those years and sexual experiences out of your memory. If those experiences were good, the memory of them will be pleasurable to you. However, that in itself can be a problem if those experiences were more rewarding to you than your present ones with your husband or wife. If your former sexual experiences were bad, then you will, no doubt, try to erase them from your mind. A good and satisfying sex life with your present spouse can certainly help achieve that goal.

One husband said, "My wife is always asking me what it was like to make love with my former wife and whether our sex life now is better. How do you answer that? Sometimes it is, and sometimes it's not so good. Should I tell her the truth each time we have sex? What good does that do?" Of course, it doesn't do any good, and it may harm your present relationship. Several husbands said that their wives had asked them similar questions.

When your partner asks about your former sexual experiences, it is always best to redirect the question into some positive and encouraging statements about your love for your present partner. Don't get into the trap of comparing sexual experiences. Tell your partner that because of the commitment you have made to him or her, the only thing that matters is your relationship now. The past is gone. We have to live in the present. Make it beautiful and loving, and the past will seem like "a long time ago." Don't tell your partner that she or he is better or worse than a former partner. Simply reassure your partner of your love and loyalty. Keep giving assurances along the way (and during sex) of how much joy you have in your sexual relationship now. Keep focusing all the attention on your present relationship, and forget the past, whether good or bad.

Most couples said that thoughts of former partners did not help them to adjust to present partners. These thoughts stand in the way. The Bible speaks of "taking every thought captive to the obedience of Christ" (2 Corinthians 10:5). That's good advice. Philippians 4:8 adds:

> Finally, brethren, whatever is true, whatever is honorable, whatever is right, whatever is pure, whatever is lovely, whatever is of good repute, if there is any excellence and if anything worthy of praise, let your mind dwell on these things.

How Do You Cope with Your Sexual Fears?

The remarried have special fears concerning sex. Several of them spoke of the fear of rejection. If it happened once before, maybe it will happen again. Some spoke of the fear of sexual inability. Because of past failures, they had much fear that they could not satisfy their partners. These people find it hard not to worry about what their partners think of their sexual performance. Was it as good as with the former spouse? Was it enough? Was there enough passion? Was the technique acceptable? You don't want to think this way, but sometimes you can't help it because of what you have experienced.

Much of this comes from the pain and hurts of divorce. One

man who left his wife for another woman said to her: "You don't satisfy me sexually. As a matter of fact, I don't think you have the ability to satisfy a man!" That terrible remark has remained with her for years. She has much difficulty relating to her present husband because of what her former spouse said to her.

If your former partner was unfaithful to you, you are not guilty—your former partner is. The guilt we experience is not ours to bear unless we have done something wrong. Only a selfish and cruel person tries to blame someone else for his own sins. The truth is, most marital partners who are unfaithful to their spouses are so because they want to be. Whatever the explanation, the Bible is quite clear on this matter. James 1:14 says, "But each one is tempted when he is carried away and enticed by *his own lust.*"

Much of our fear could be eliminated by a constant dose of God's love. When a marital partner truly loves his or her spouse, it won't matter how the spouse "performs" sexually. God's love is much stronger than that. It does not depend upon sexual performance or technique. If you want things differently, then say so. Don't make your partner wonder all the time as to whether you are satisfied or not. That's not only unloving and selfish of you, it's cruel and damaging to your partner's sense of self-worth.

One remarried husband said to me, "Pastor, my wife thinks that having sex once a month is all that we need. She said that her first husband was 'sex-crazy' and that that was the reason he was unfaithful to her. Her view is that you can have 'too much sex.' She says it's not good for you." I asked him what he thought about it. He said, "I'm not sex-crazy, but I sure need more than I'm getting!" I said, "Have you talked with her about it?" He said, "No. I don't want her to think of me as she does her former husband." I said, "You'd better stop worrying about that, and begin to share openly with her about your needs and how much you need her help." He was surprised to find her so receptive when he told her he needed more sex. She said, "Why didn't you say so?" She told him that she was ready every night if he needed it. Needless to say, they are getting along much better these days.

Most remarried couples spoke of their hesitancy to tell their partners about their sexual desires and needs. They all seemed to manifest a certain degree of insecurity. None of them wanted to lose what he or she now has. The past looms large. They all try to cope with the problem from within, often asking God for more strength. While this is commendable, the best solution is to tell your partner openly what you desire and need.

A man in my office one day was telling me he needed much more sex from his wife than he was getting. I said, "Have you told her this?" He said, "Well, not in so many words. But, she should get the point!" I said, "Why don't you call her right now and tell her." He said, "Right now?" I said, "Right now!" He nervously picked up the phone and called his wife. He said, "Honey, I just wanted you to know that I need more sex from you than I'm getting." She said, "You get home right now—we'll take care of that!" He smiled, and left the office without his coat.

What If Your Partner Does Not Respond?

Don't give up. That's what usually happens after time goes by. You lose hope that your partner will ever change. One wife said, "I have asked him (her husband) many times about having sex more often, and he says that he doesn't need it. When I told him that I needed it, he told me to go take a cold shower and leave him alone." I felt sorry for her, and called her husband and confronted him. He started to get mad on the phone. I said, "Bob, you are disobeying the clear teaching of the Bible (1 Corinthians 7:1–5). Your problem is not with me, it's with God Himself!" A few weeks later he called me and thanked me for confronting him, but here's what he said: "I know my wife needs more sex than I'm giving, but I just don't feel like doing it most of the time." I told him that he was commanded by God to do it for his wife even if he didn't feel like it. If I waited to do things only when I felt like it, I wouldn't get much of anything done. I told him that his responsibility was to obey God. He said, "But how do I get up for it when I'm not stimulated?" I said, "It's not necessary. The important thing is for you to minister to your wife. Stop thinking about yourself. Use your head—there are many ways to bring sexual enjoyment to your wife, regardless of how stimulated you are."

The conclusion to the above story is quite interesting. What his wife discovered she really needed was his constant affection for her. She didn't need the "bed" so much as she needed his loving embraces and touch. Often the little expressions of physical affection during each day are the things that bring the abiding sense of satisfaction and pleasure.

We must not oversimplify the problems which many partners have in this regard. It is frustrating and extremely discouraging when your marital partner does not respond to you sexually. If you are a Christian, you know that it is wrong to satisfy your desires outside of marriage, but you are often tempted to do so because of your partner's lack of response.

In addition to talking to your partner about it (read Proverbs 27:5, 6), do not underestimate the power of prayer. One wife shared with me her joy over how God was answering prayer. She had a very unresponsive husband, and she made a commitment with God to pray about it every hour during the day. When the clock struck 9:00 A.M., she would pray. When it was 10:00 A.M., she prayed again, and so on throughout the day. Within a few weeks, her husband began to respond to her in a new way. Later, she found out that he had gone to a Christian bookstore and picked up a copy of a marriage book that started him to think about his lack of response. She was so excited to learn that he had done that during one of her days of constant prayer. Without her saying a word to her husband, God had changed his heart and used a Christian book to get him going. That's much better than pinning a note to his shirt, or leaving another marriage book in the bathroom, or a note on the refrigerator saying, "Have you hugged your wife today?"

The Desire to Please Your Partner

Once you remarry, don't give up in your desires to please your partner. We all know how easy it is to take our partners for granted. We stop being romantic, and we stop thinking of ways to please each other. When your partner knows that you want to please him or her, it definitely turns the sexual thermometer up!

One husband called me and shared this cute story about what his wife did to liven up their marriage. They were both married previously and those marriages were sad and tragic. They were now very happy as a married couple, but their sexual relationship was quite platonic and routine. She decided to do something about it. One day she called him at his office and said, "Honey, the kids will be staying at Grandma's tonight, and I thought we might have a little candlelight dinner here at the house for just the two of us. Does that sound good to you?" He said, "Sure—that's OK."

She then said, "I've been thinking about what to wear, and I can't find anything in the closet, so I'm just running around the house now without any clothes on! Oh, by the way, I just made a commitment to do whatever you would like to do in the way of sex. It's your night, and I'll do anything you want me to do. Well, I know you have to get back to work, so take your time, and when you get home I'll be ready." He said, "Pastor, there's no way I could work the rest of that afternoon. I couldn't wait to get home. I could hardly believe that my wife had said what she did." Needless to say, their sexual life got a "booster shot."

When you seek to please your partner rather than yourself, things will change. When you are trying to motivate your partner to change because of your own needs, your partner usually will resist or at least be slow at responding. That's the way human nature works.

In some respects, the principles that apply to all married couples concerning sex, also apply to remarried couples. Don't dwell on your unique situation. We all have problems, and we all must make our own sexual adjustments. Remarried couples must face the past and deal with it. Don't let the past control your relationships in the present. The Bible teaches us that "perfect (mature) love casts out fear" (1 John 4:18). Your fears can be eliminated by God's wonderful love, produced by the Holy Spirit of God. Paul said in 2 Timothy 1:7, "For God has not given us a spirit of timidity (fear), but of power and love and discipline."

Questions for Reflection

1. What should you do about thoughts of your sex life with your former partner?
2. What are some of your "sexual fears"?
3. How can these "sexual fears" be eliminated in time?
4. What should you do if your partner does not respond to your sexual desires and needs?
5. How important is your desire to please your partner?
6. What can you do that you know will please your partner?

Part II

The Strategies of Remarriage

"What therefore God has joined together, let no man separate."

—Matthew 19:6

"With men this is impossible, but with God all things are possible"

—Matthew 19:26

"It is better that you should not vow than that you should vow and not pay."

—Ecclesiastes 5:5

7

Learn to Forgive

In most serious counseling sessions I have had with remarried couples, the problem of forgiveness comes up. And I have learned that many of the guilt feelings which these people have experienced are rooted in two areas—their inability to accept God's forgiveness for past failures or their inability to forgive people in situations where they have been hurt. Usually these feelings are directed toward former partners.

Why do we have difficulty forgiving others? I have discovered at least four reasons in my discussions with remarried people.

Emotional Hurts

These hurts run deep. Some days you think you have the victory over a personal hurt that happened in the past, and then on other days it affects you all over again. When your marital partner has done something to hurt you deeply, it is very difficult for you to forgive. It's easy to fight back when you've been wounded; our hurts can become barriers to true forgiveness.

Bob Lausen had been married to his wife Ann for about three years when he came home one day and said, "I need to talk to you, Ann, about something that's been happening to me at work." Ann was not ready for what Bob told her. "There's a girl in the office that I've been seeing lately, and she really turns me on." Ann was stunned. "What are you trying to say, Bob?" "I'm sorry, Ann, but I think I want a divorce." Ann began to cry. She could not believe what he was saying. "Why, Bob? What have I done to make you want someone else?" Bob said, "You just don't meet my needs like this girl does." Ann snapped back, "You mean you've already been having sex with her?" Bob answered "Yes, and it's pretty exciting to me. This girl and I really have something going!" Ann could not believe that it was happening to her.

In the months that followed, Ann wavered between feelings of inadequacy and feelings of bitterness toward Bob. He filed for a divorce, and soon married that girl. Ann was still hurt and filled with guilt feelings. She had done nothing wrong, but she still felt guilty. She had been deeply hurt, and it would take some time for her to recover.

There is a sense in which we are all inadequate and unable to meet the needs of our partners. Without God's help, none of us would make it. However, Ann's former husband was justifying his sinful desires by making Ann feel that she was inadequate to meet his needs. Ann was not guilty; Bob was.

Two years later, Ann married a wonderful Christian man who truly loves her. But her emotional hurt was very deep and often she would think of Bob and literally be filled with anger toward him. She could not forgive him for what he had done to her. The sad truth is that her emotional hurt was being carried over into her second marriage.

When your partner has done something to hurt you deeply, it is very difficult to forgive. If you are a Christian, you know that God wants you to forgive, but it still does not come easily. Much of the problem lies in your interpretation of what happened. Ann felt angry because what Bob did reflected on her sexual capacity. She kept wondering how the other girl looked and what she was like. These comparisons were not helping her to forgive Bob for what he had done. Ann finally came to the realization that she was not guilty, and that the problem was Bob's old sin nature. His lust had gotten the best of him, and he deliberately sinned against God and against Ann. When Ann saw his offense as primarily against God, she began to feel compassion toward Bob and desired to forgive him.

If you are hurting over something your present or former partner has said or done, one of the best things to do is pray. I know that sounds simplistic. But it's true. Prayer is recommended in James 5:13 for those who are emotionally upset. It is better to pour out your heart to the Lord than to others. The Bible says in 1 Peter 5:7, "Casting all your anxiety upon Him, because He cares for you." Do as the songwriter says, "Take your burden to the Lord and leave it there."

Secondly, read passages in the Bible which have to do with God's love and forgiveness. I have found the Psalms to be comforting and encouraging when I have been emotionally hurt.

Another thing you can do is write down on a piece of paper exactly what was done or said and make a list of what steps to take to resolve those things. Settle what you can right away. If it is too late to take care of some things, then thank the Lord, recognize His sovereignty over all things, and stop worrying about them.

No matter what hurts we may feel over the things our partners have said or done, the Bible teaches us to take it patiently and that this pleases God. Matthew 5:10–12 tells us that our reward in heaven will be great, especially when we have been falsely accused, slandered, or mistreated. If what your partner has said about you is true, then it is no special thing for you to take it gracefully. You deserved it. But, when you suffer unjustly and are accused falsely, and you refuse to retaliate or seek revenge, this finds favor with God and brings great reward from Him. Learn to leave these matters with the justice of God. He'll take care of it in time.

Repeated Offenses

When a person keeps doing the same thing over and over again, it becomes increasingly difficult to forgive.

Alice Smith is a good friend of ours. She calls my wife often concerning her husband David. When he first committed adultery, it was hard on Alice, but she learned to forgive him for what he had done. The real trouble came when Alice discovered that he had committed adultery several times after that incident. David has a way of confessing that draws you to him. You feel sincerely sorry for him, and you want to give him another chance. Alice is growing weary of his unfaithfulness, and is very close to divorcing him. My wife asked me to talk with her. What I found on the phone was a bitter woman. She said, "Pastor, David continues to commit adultery, and I've had it with him. I know we're supposed to forgive, but after all, how many times do I have to take him back?" I said, "Alice, you know what Jesus said." "I know—seventy times seven!" I understood her reluctance to forgive him, and I also knew him well enough to know how he manipulates people with insincere confession and insufficient repentance. I decided to confront him about it.

When I finally got to talk to David, he was very defensive. He tried to explain his problem, but the longer he talked, the more I was convinced he was trying to deceive me. I finally blurted out, "David, are you having sex again with someone other than Alice?" He quickly spoke, "Who told you?" I said, "No one. But obviously you are." For the next two hours he received some unwelcome advice from me. I told him that I could no longer fellowship with him if he continued his immorality. I told him that the Bible encourages me to treat him like an unbeliever because of his conduct. I also said that his continued adultery without sincere repentance was grounds enough for Alice to divorce him.

This story, unfortunately, does not have a happy ending. Alice divorced David, and before long he married a woman with whom he had been having an affair for some time. I'm sure you realize how difficult it is for Alice to forgive him. When he was unfaithful to her the first time, she responded well though she was deeply hurt. Alice still struggles with forgiveness. I don't blame her for that, but I do know that we all must learn to forgive even when the offense is repeated many times. In many ways, that is the acid test of our ability to forgive.

In Matthew 18:21, 22, Peter said, " 'Lord, how often shall my brother sin against me and I forgive him? Up to seven times?' Jesus said to him, 'I do not say to you, up to seven times, but up to seventy times seven!' " That's the standard for all of us to apply.

A friend of my wife's came by our house one day just before noon. I had come home that day for lunch. She wanted to talk about her marriage. She was having a great struggle with her husband's attitudes toward her and her children. Both she and her husband had previously been divorced and she was quite discouraged when she said, "He's always condemning us for our failures. I don't think I can stand it anymore!" I talked with her briefly about forgiveness, and she said, "That's what bothers me. He realizes what he has done when I confront him about it, and quickly asks me for forgiveness. As soon as that incident is over, there's another one. There's no relief from it. He just keeps on doing it." She asked if I would talk to him, and I said I would.

The following week, both of them were at our home for dessert and coffee after a special meeting at church. I said to him, "Why do you feel it necessary to point out the faults of your wife and children?" He didn't get mad; he immediately started to apologize for his actions. I said, "What good is it to keep saying you're sorry if you turn right around and do it again?" I told him that it was becoming very difficult for his wife to forgive him because he was continuing to do it.

Until that night, I don't think he realized how often he was doing this. One of the best things he did was to ask his wife to pray for him and to bring it to his attention the moment he started to do it again. He told her that he was determined to gain the victory over it. Needless to say, she was really happy.

I've got some bad habits that need to be changed, and I'm sure you do also. We all have areas of our lives that need to be changed. But in the meantime, we need to forgive. My wife tolerates some of my habits, and is an example of forgiveness to me. I usually throw my sweaty clothes on the floor of our utility room where the washer and dryer are. Since I play racquetball and handball two or three times a week, this is a regular occurrence. Finally, my wife said, "Sweetheart, do you think you could put those athletic clothes of yours in the clothes basket rather than on the floor?" Until she said that, I didn't appreciate how she felt. It didn't take too much effort on my part to put them in the clothes basket instead of throwing them on the floor. The thing that amazed me was her patience. I said, "How long have you wanted me to do that?" She said, "For years." I said, "Honey, I'm really sorry. You should have said something." She said, "That's okay. I forgive you." Short and sweet. What an example she is to me.

Wrong Standards of Evaluation

One of the most common reasons why we have difficulty forgiving our marital partners is that we use the wrong standard of evaluating each other. The normal way we evaluate something is how we feel about it and our feelings become the basis for determining our forgiveness.

This is so obvious in counseling situations. The words, "I feel" crop up continually. We often relate to each other only on the basis of how we feel about what was said or done. In a particular counseling session with a lady who was having trouble forgiving her husband for his actions and attitudes, over twenty times in the course of our conversation she referred to how she "felt" about what he was doing. I counted them! I should have concentrated more on what she was saying, but her constant reference to feelings made me start counting! I said to her, "Do you realize how often you have referred to your feelings about your husband?" She said, "What difference does that make? That's how I feel about him." I said, "You did it again." She said, "Did what?" "Refer to your feelings." She said, "What is your point, Pastor?" I tried to explain. "I think you are evaluating your husband by how you feel, and not by the actual facts. You even told me that though you did not have any facts, this was the way you felt about him."

Like so many of us, she was unaware of how her feelings were controlling her response to her husband. The incidents that she referred to that made it difficult for her to forgive him were really quite insignificant. Her feelings made more of the situation than the facts warranted.

When I'm tired and weary, I don't feel too forgiving. I make small incidents seem like colossal problems. It's hard to be objective when you are physically exhausted. Because I feel bad physically, I start feeling bad emotionally toward every little thing that happens. Instead of applying God's forgiveness, I make a big deal out of it.

The real standard for forgiveness is not what we feel, but the example of Jesus Christ. No matter how we feel about something that was said or done, when we look at how Jesus Christ forgives, we are compelled to forgive others. Consider how often the Bible teaches us to forgive as Jesus Christ has forgiven us.

Ephesians 4:32 says:

> And be kind to one another, tender-hearted, forgiving each other, just as God in Christ also has forgiven you.

Colossians 3:13 adds:

> Bearing with one another, and forgiving each other, whoever has a complaint against anyone; just as the Lord forgave you, so also should you.

Judgmental Attitude

It's easy to be self-righteous, especially if you have avoided certain sins which society treats as serious. When your sins are private, and not public, it's also easy to be judgmental of others. When you think you would never do what your partner has done, then it's a simple matter to understand your judgmental spirit. Matthew 7:1, 2 says:

> Do not judge lest you be judged yourselves. For in the way you judge, you will be judged; and by your standard of measure, it will be measured to you.

When your partner's failures improve the opinion you have of yourself, then you will have great difficulty forgiving and forgetting. Christ condemned self-righteousness in Luke 18:9–14. He spoke of a religious leader who prayed, "God, I thank Thee that I am not like other people: swindlers, unjust, adulterers, or even like this tax-gatherer." Jesus said, "for everyone who exalts himself shall be humbled. . . ."

When your partner's failures decrease your concern for your own faults, you will fall into a judgmental attitude. Romans 2:1–3 makes this clear when it says:

> Therefore you are without excuse, every man of you who passes judgment, for in that you judge another, you condemn yourself; for you who judge practice the same things. And we know that the judgment of God rightly falls upon those who practice such things. And do you suppose this, O man, when you pass judgment upon those who practice such things and do the same yourself, that you will escape the judgment of God?

The answer to that last question in Romans 2:3 is that we will not escape God's judgment. A judgmental spirit will keep you from forgiving your partner and it is often seen when your partner's faults become your main concern rather than your own.

John was a good man and tried to be a good husband, but his big problem was his constant concern over his wife's faults. I said to him one day, "John, your wife can't be that bad." I asked him, "What are your faults?" He said, "Well, I probably have some, but I have learned to control them." His pride made me thankful I wasn't married to him. It's difficult to live with someone who continually points out your faults and never sees his own.

Another common hindrance to a forgiving spirit is the desire to see your partner punished for what he or she has done. We should leave that matter to God, but unfortunately, that is not always the case. I cannot help thinking about the story in John 8:1–11, of the woman taken in adultery. They were ready to stone her, but Jesus said, "He who is without sin among you, let him be the first to throw a stone at her."

One lady I know refuses to have sex with her husband, when she knows he really wants it, as a way of punishing him. She feels that she is fully justified in this because of her husband's past sins. Little does she realize that she is also sinning against the clear teaching of 1 Corinthians 7:5.

Another example of a judgmental spirit that is such a hindrance to forgiving and forgetting is for a marital partner to tell others about the sins and faults of the other partner. This is an extremely dangerous habit. We have all seen couples do this and we can feel the tension when it happens. First Peter 4:8 says, "Above all, keep fervent in your love for one another, because love covers a multitude of sins." Proverbs 17:9 adds, "He who covers a transgression seeks love, but he who repeats a matter separates intimate friends."

I well remember the look of hurt in my wife's eyes when I shared what I thought was an amusing incident that happened to her. The problem was that it pointed out one of her faults. The moment I said it, I knew I was wrong. I'm guilty of far more problems in that area than she. We often make remarks about the faults of our partners in the very areas where we ourselves are having difficulty.

When the failure of your partner prompts you to review his past and emphasize additional failures, then you have a judgmental spirit and will find it difficult to forgive and forget. Thank the Lord for what Isaiah 43:25 says—"I, even I, am the one who wipes out your transgressions for My own sake; and I will not remember your sins." Psalms 103:12 states, "As far as the east is from the west, so far has He removed our transgressions from us." Don't bring up the past. If it has been confessed and resolved, then leave it alone. Bringing up past failures only increases the barriers to real forgiveness. There is so much in each of our lives that we need to forgive and forget. Once you have said that you have forgiven your partner, don't ever bring that particular issue up again.

How to Forgive and Forget

These seven steps do not cover everything that needs to be said. But, if followed, they will go a long way in helping us all to forgive and forget.

1. *Recognize the sovereignty and purpose of God in everything that has happened.*

God tells us that He is working "all things" for our good (Romans 8:28) and that He is personally involved in the "all things" of our lives (Romans 11:33–36; Ephesians 1:11). We need to rest in His knowledge and plan for us. He knows what is best and He is fully aware of why these things have happened to us. He wants our good. He wants to bless us more than we want to receive it.

I mentioned that fact to Dick Jones one day because he was so emotionally disturbed over his past divorce and the present problems he was having with his new wife. He said that the thought of God's sovereignty was definitely *not* on his mind. He found it hard to be thankful. But he does need to move in that direction. We too must learn to thank the Lord for whatever problems we have had, knowing that the Lord will use all of them to make us what He wants us to be and ultimately bring our good and His glory out of them.

2. *Reflect on the forgiveness of Christ and how He would handle such things.*

Our hesitation in forgiving is often rooted in our neglect of the Word of God which teaches the forgiveness of Christ. The more I learn of how Christ would react, the better prepared I am to react to others.

One wife told me that a book she read on forgiveness literally changed her attitude about her past divorce. Her guilt was enormous, even though her husband had committed immorality and there were righteous grounds for her divorce. But when she stopped to think of Christ's forgiveness, she found it in her heart to forgive her former husband.

3. *Realize your own sinfulness and the potential of sinning in the same way.*

Here is a real problem for most of us. Our reluctance to forgive others is often evidence of our being blind to our sinfulness. Galatians 6:1 says:

> Brethren, even if a man is caught in any trespass, you who are spiritual, restore such a one in a spirit of gentleness; looking to yourselves, lest you too be tempted.

That "looking to yourself" must always be there. A forgiving heart is well aware of its own weaknesses. It does not parade its good points, nor ignore its faults. Under the right provocation, each of us is capable of the greatest of sins. How we need the grace and forgiveness of Christ! Don't accuse your partner and ignore the sin in your own heart.

4. *Reevaluate your responsibility in each matter.*

Let's face it—there really are two sides to every story. Before you resist forgiving and forgetting, think for a moment about your own responsibility. Matthew 7:3 warns us about judging others and not dealing with our own problems. It says:

> And why do you look at the speck that is in your brother's eye, but do not notice the log that is in your own eye?

We are told to get rid of the "log" in our own eye first.

Mary kept telling me about the sins of her husband. Somehow

in the conversation I kept getting the feeling that I was hearing only one side of the story. When I asked her what her husband would say about all of this, she responded, "He would say that I'm to blame." I said, "Why would he say that?" She then proceeded to give me about three or four things that her husband would say were wrong with her attitudes. When I asked, "Is this true about you?" she said, "Yes, but that isn't the problem—he is!"

While we may easily see another person's problem, we may not see our own. Before you start blaming your partner, learn to evaluate your own responsibility first. Ask the Lord to show you those attitudes and actions in your own life that need to be changed.

5. *Remember your commitment and vows.*

Commitment is the foundation of marriage. You said, "in sickness and in health" and "till death do us part." Did you mean that when you said it? Doesn't our commitment demand our forgiveness? When you pledged yourself to your marital partner, didn't that involve a willingness to forgive and forget? Didn't you realize there would be points of conflict and argument in your marriage? If we are to forgive and forget, we must remember the commitment we made to each other. Staying with it when you're tempted to "throw in the towel" is what your commitment means. How can we forgive if we are not totally committed?

In the heat of argument and disagreement, too many partners threaten to leave and get a divorce. Is that remembering the vows? Those kinds of threats become barriers to a willingness to forgive and forget.

A husband friend of mine shared that he could not take his wife's attitudes any more. Both of them had been married before, and their marriage to each other has been far from perfect. Lots of arguments exist in their lives with very little forgiveness. I asked him about the vow he had made. He said that she had gone too far, and he wasn't going to take it any more. But again I asked about his vow and whether he had spoken that vow before God. The longer we talked, the more he realized that his vow must lead to a forgiving attitude and a loyalty to his wife no matter what she does or says.

6. *Respond immediately upon your partner's confession and repentance.*

It's hard to forgive if there's no true confession and repentance. Luke 17:3, 4 says:

> Be on your guard! If your brother sins, rebuke him; and if he repents, forgive him. And if he sins against you seven times a day, and returns to you seven times, saying, "I repent," forgive him.

Repentance is a condition for forgiveness; otherwise, the forgiveness is not based on solid ground. If we have done wrong, then we should confess and forsake that wrong if we expect our partners to forgive us.

One of the difficulties we face is when our partners repent and ask for our forgiveness and we do not respond with love and acceptance. That really hurts. The Bible says that we are to forgive the moment repentance takes place.

Kathy was hurt, and her husband felt shame for what he had done. He confessed his sin to her, and asked for her forgiveness. She refused. Their marriage got worse, but she convinced herself that it was his fault, not hers. She failed to see her problem. She refused to respond in love and forgiveness to her husband when he repented. Matthew 6:14, 15 speaks to this:

> For if you forgive men for their transgressions, your heavenly Father will also forgive you. But if you do not forgive men, then your Father will not forgive your transgressions.

7. *Reassure your partner of your love and acceptance.*

If you truly have a forgiving and forgetting attitude, you will do what you can to reassure your partner of your love and acceptance. As Christ has accepted us, so we are to respond to one another (Romans 15:7).

The Book of 1 Corinthians includes a discussion about one of their members who was guilty of incest (chapter 5). Paul admonishes them to exercise discipline by putting the erring brother out of their fellowship. By the time Paul wrote 2 Corinthians, the sinning brother had repented. Paul wrote these words in 2 Corinthians 2:6–8:

> Sufficient for such a one is this punishment which was inflicted by the majority, so that on the contrary you should rather forgive and comfort him, lest somehow such a one be overwhelmed by excessive sorrow. Wherefore I urge you to reaffirm your love for him.

That story speaks to all of us. When your partner seeks your forgiveness and truly confesses and repents of wrongdoing, then immediately show your love and complete acceptance. WE MUST LEARN TO FORGIVE AND FORGET.

Questions for Reflection

1. Give four reasons why it is so difficult to forgive.
2. What can be done to relieve a deep emotional hurt?
3. What standard should be used in forgiving your partner?
4. In what ways can we recognize a judgmental attitude?
5. What steps are necessary in order to forgive and forget?
6. Is there a situation in your marriage for which you find it hard to forgive your partner or former partner? What do you plan to do about it?

8

Love Those Kids!

The real trouble in remarriage is not the divorce or the former partner. It is learning how to deal with a child who is not your own. We have discussed some of the basic needs of stepchildren. Learning to handle them is truly a difficult assignment. In this chapter we want to explore some of the practical problems which remarried couples have to face in trying to raise children who are not their own. Hopefully, through the experiences of others, you will learn some things that will help you.

Problem No. 1—Whose Child?

Many remarried couples have shared with me that one of the first questions that must be settled is who gets the children, and how they are to be regarded by the stepparent in particular.

An article appearing in the *Long Beach Independent Press-Telegram* (Calif.) on December 3, 1981 exposed some of the feelings of stepparents regarding their relationships to their stepchildren. The article was entitled: "It's tough being a stepmom!" The writer said:

Instead of gathering at dinner each evening to share the triumphs of our separate days, we slugged it out at the table over when she (teenage stepdaughter) had gotten in the night before, whether or not she would be allowed to go out that night, what classes she had cut that day, and how many failure notices we had gotten from her teachers. Instead of cozy family chats about current events, we had fights about things like whether I felt I was doing the kid a favor by letting her live with us (I did); whether she was going to treat us as she treated her mother (she tried); and whether my husband was going to get tough with "his" kid (he tried).

A stepmother spends a lot of time, before she learns to relax, worrying over little things that I am sure real mothers don't give a second thought to.

Most of the experts dealing with stepparents and stepchildren agree that the problem of failed expectations is common and serious. People believe that everything will be OK and it usually isn't.

For the stepmother, the children are part of an earlier commitment her husband shared with someone else. Most second wives don't really like to think about their predecessors, but children make that impossible to avoid. His kids are her emissaries in your house!

Near the end of her article she wrote:

Not only was I being less than the perfect mother, but these youngsters I had wanted to rescue sometimes needed rescuing from me. That realization made me feel terrible at times.

When this lady said "we had fights about things like whether I felt I was doing the kid a favor by letting her live with us (I did)," she was expressing what many stepparents feel. It is difficult to take a child that is not your own and to start relating to that child as though he or she belonged to you.

These questions dealing with the relationship of a stepchild to a stepparent must be clearly dealt with before the marriage takes place. This is the consensus among several remarried couples with whom I have talked, some of whom did not resolve these matters before remarriage. As a result, they have had many difficulties. It is not enough to say, "It will all work out in time." Rather, time must be taken to resolve these questions before you remarry.

When divorce occurs, the ability of the husband and wife to think clearly and sensibly about the children is restricted and limited by their emotional involvement. When one partner simply does not want the children, then the decision concerning custody is relatively easy to make. But when there are more children than one stepparent can handle, it becomes an issue. This is especially true when there are more than two children and the husband says he cannot take care of any of them, and the wife, on limited income, must bear the responsibility of them all. If the children are quite young, the problem is intensified. In our ministry with stepparents, and especially with single parents, we have discovered much bitterness over this issue.

Normally, wives feel a greater burden to care for the children. Husbands should accept full responsibility and accountability for this matter as well, but such is often not the case. If the couple who is divorcing has more than two children, it is best to divide the responsibilities between the husband and wife, at least until the financial and personal care of the children can be adequately worked out. Of course, the real losers in divorce proceedings that involve the care of the children are the children themselves.

On many occasions, the divorcing couple will fight over the custody of the children. This becomes a major issue in terms of guilt and freedom. Sometimes the emotional love of the parent for the child is a substitute for the emotional hurt which results from the marital partner leaving.

If a couple who is divorcing really cares about the children, we would recommend that they seek the services of a Christian arbitrator. If there is a Christian lawyer available, who has the time and burden for this kind of ministry, such a person would be best. The couple, of course, must be willing to submit to the counsel and decisions of such arbitrators. When they do, many of the problems regarding custody can be decided satisfactorily.

I believe that the Bible teaches that believers should handle their difficulties with other believers and not go before unbelievers for solutions. In 1 Corinthians 6:1–8, we have these remarkable words:

> Does any one of you, when he has a case against his neighbor, dare to go to law before the unrighteous, and not before the saints? Or do you not know that the saints will judge the world? And if the world is judged by you, are you not competent to constitute the smallest law courts? Do you not know that we shall judge angels? How much more, matters of this life? If then you have law courts dealing with matters of this life, do you appoint them as judges who are of no account in the church? I say this to your shame. Is it so, that there is not among you one wise man who will be able to decide between his brethren, but brother goes to law with brother, and that before unbelievers? Actually, then, it is already a defeat for you, that you have lawsuits with one another. Why not rather be wronged? Why not rather be defrauded? On the contrary, you yourselves wrong and defraud, and that your brethren.

Why not allow your Christian brothers and sisters to settle these matters for you? Are you afraid to submit to the authority and decision-making of believers? Would they be less compassionate toward you than unbelievers? Would they care less about your children than unbelievers in a secular court of law? Many people think that it is required to settle these matters in a secular court room. That simply is not true. These matters can be settled out of court before individuals who are properly accepted and designated by the people involved as arbitrators.

When the children are young (preschool or elementary age), it is usually best for them to live with their mother rather than their father. It is best, in any case, to establish a permanent situation and not be bouncing the child or children back and forth between the former parents. If the children are teenagers, they should be brought into the discussions regarding custody even though it is hard for them to be objective. Often the divorcing parents do not want to talk to their children at any length about the divorce and custody matters because the children become emotional and will usually appeal to their parents to get back together.

When Ed and Carol tried to discuss their divorce and custody matters with their two teenagers, it became quite an emotional battle. Their junior high girl could not stop weeping and told them that she wanted to live with them both and couldn't understand why they couldn't work their problems out and stay married. Their teenage son, who was a sophomore in high school, said very little, but they knew it was affecting him greatly. When they asked him with whom he would like to live, he refused to answer. He said nothing. He just left the room. Getting mad at him (which is what Ed did) didn't help. After all, it was not his fault that his parents were getting a divorce.

When this son found out that Ed was interested in marrying another woman, he was deeply hurt. Immediately he knew that he wanted to live with his mother. Ed loved his boy, but he knew that his son could not accept his affair with this other woman. The relationship between Ed and his son has been strained ever since and the son carries a deep bitterness in his heart toward Ed. The daughter is now a senior in high school. She still prays for her daddy to come home, even though he remarried. Carol has never remarried.

How should the stepparent respond?

After careful and prayerful discussions about child custody, how does a stepparent respond to the children he or she will inherit as a result of a remarriage? Assuming that there has been a complete airing of the potential problems, and that the stepparent is not only willing but excited with the new responsibilities he or she will have with stepchildren, how should the stepparent respond to the stepchild? Answer: very carefully!

New stepparents should not demand that the child call them "Dad" or "Mother." If the child is of preschool age, it will come easier. Elementary children will have tremendous emotional conflicts over what to call their stepparents, especially if their relationship has been good with their real parents. Teenagers should be given the freedom to call the stepparents by their first names if they do not feel comfortable referring to them as "Dad" and "Mother." If you make this a big issue, it could be a sore point in the years ahead. Deal with it gradually and lovingly. Take time to talk about it with your stepchildren. Explain how much you love them and would like to relate to them as a real parent would. You have to earn that kind of respect and loving relationship. It cannot be forced upon them. If you do force it you will regret it.

One remarried husband friend of ours shared with us the sad story of how he tried to have his stepson call him "Dad." The boy was only eight years old when his mother married this man, and the stepdad kept insisting that he call him "Dad" whenever addressing him. One day when his stepdad tried to discipline him for something that he did, the little boy stuck his fist in his stepdad's face and said, "My dad told me that I didn't have to call you 'Dad,' and that if I ever did, he would never come to see me again!" Naturally, the boy could not handle such rejection by his real father, so he had determined not to give in to his stepdad's demands. Of course, it is tragic that any parent would say things like this to a child. Such remarks can only make the task of the stepparents more difficult.

One good thing a stepparent can do is to teach the stepchild from the Bible about the subject of adoption. This is a wonderful message for stepchildren to hear. All believers in Jesus Christ have been "adopted" into God's family (Ephesians 1:5; Galatians 4:5; Romans 8:15–17). The Bible teaches that we have a special relationship to God because of His adopting us. Romans 8:15 says we can cry out "Abba! Father!" The word "Abba" is an Aramaic expression a child would use in calling his father. It is a word indicating intimacy and closeness. Even though we are adopted into God's family, the Bible teaches (Romans 8:17) that we are treated as full "heirs of God" and "fellow heirs with Christ." The stepparent can continually assure his or her stepchildren that they are full-fledged members of the family.

I really liked what one friend told me he does with his stepson every night. He goes into his room, reads a chapter from the Bible, kneels down beside his bed and prays, and then gives his stepson a big hug and kiss, and says, "I know it's hard for you to call me your dad, but I do understand. I love you just as if you were my real son, and if you don't mind, I'm going to call you 'son' because that's how I really feel about you!" Within a few months, his stepson was responding freely to him as though he were his real father. By the way, he still calls him "Dad."

Problem No. 2—How Do You Discipline a Stepchild?

Remarried couples speak of this problem often. It is much easier to show love and affection than it is to discipline. I don't know why this is true, but most stepparents are too lenient with the stepchildren. Perhaps we don't feel that we have the right to discipline the stepchild because he or she is not our own natural offspring. Maybe the problem lies in the fear of rejection and rebellion. We don't want to experience any of the "horror stories" we have heard other remarried people tell of rebellious stepchildren.

Whatever the reason for the leniency of stepparents, it is unwise. It creates more problems than it avoids. If you have decided to accept the responsibility of stepparenting, then along with that comes the task of discipline. It is not an option which you can take or leave. It is your solemn responsibility before God. A lack of discipline will cause greater problems to the child than whatever trauma is caused by discipline.

When you inherit stepchildren in a remarriage, it is important for you and your mate to lay down some guidelines and rules for the management of the home and the exercise of discipline. Don't use the "trial and error" method of raising your stepchildren. Agree with your marital partner ahead of time as to what procedures you will follow in case of offenses. If the two of you are not in agreement, then further problems will result. The disciplining of children is not easy even when the children are your own. It's much more difficult when you try to discipline stepchildren.

Ted was having great difficulty disciplining his two stepchildren. He and his wife, Angela, had been married for about two years. Angela's children were of preschool age when she married Ted. Ted had no children from his previous marriage, so, in a sense, he was like a new father. Of course, Ted was handicapped by the fact that he had not been with those children during their preschool years. Now they were both in elementary school, one in first grade, and one in second grade. Ted's thinking about discipline differed from Angela's. She felt that Ted should spank the children, but he was more lenient. When the children began having problems in school, the teacher asked for a conference with Ted and Angela. From that teacher Ted learned the necessity of disciplining the children. He recognized that day that he was wrong and entirely too tolerant of their rebellious attitudes. Now he had to correct his practices with the children and explain to them why things were going to be different.

He told me that the first time he had to spank one of his little girls was the hardest experience he had ever had. He cried and had tremendous guilt feelings over what he had done. Angela told him that he had done the right thing and urged him to be sure that he was consistent the next time he had to exercise discipline. The "next time" came the following day with the other child. She said, "You're not my daddy!" He said, "Oh yes I am!" She said, "No you're not!" He said, "Bend over!" She said, "I don't have to!" He grabbed her and turned her across his knee and spanked her. She cried for about an hour. Later that evening, she climbed into his lap while he was watching TV and said, "Thank you, Daddy, for spanking me. I really needed it!"

Yes, your children do need discipline. It is a key to their further growth and development. Obedience to authority is fundamental to great leadership in the future. You are hurting your children if you do not discipline them. They need to have responsive hearts and attitudes to authority in their lives, especially toward their stepparents.

What About Teenagers?

When your children grow older, discipline changes from spanking to other forms of restriction. They still need to learn what the guidelines are; rules need to be clearly spelled out, and reinforced from time to time. Discuss these things openly with your teenagers. Although you must make the final decisions, your teenagers will appreciate your willingness to get their viewpoints on discipline. Ask them what they would do if they were in your place.

Couples who have inherited children in their teens have all spoken a great deal about the difficulties they have. If the emotional scars of a divorce are still deep in the teenager's heart, there is going to be a struggle between that teenager and his or her stepparent over who is in charge, and why. The best way to handle this difficult situation is to sit down and talk things out. Don't assume that everything is going to be all right. Your teenage stepchild needs some time to respond to you. There are many questions in your teenager's mind about you and whether you are going to be in the home permanently. If a previous parent left, maybe you will leave also! How can he or she really trust you? You appear to be the outsider, invading the home. You sometimes are the enemy to your teenage stepchild. You may not like that, but it is often the case.

Whatever you do, go slowly. Don't push and shove your way around, demanding respect and submission. It doesn't work. Teenagers are going through the transition from being a child to becoming an adult. They want and deserve respect and treatment as adults, but they still need understanding and compassion as though they were still children. Give them room to breathe and respect their desire for privacy.

A good tactic with stepchildren in their teenage years is to ask for their help and advice. Let them know that you are new to stepparenting and that you would really appreciate their help. Try to find out their emotional hurts as soon as possible, and offer comfort, counsel, and prayer. The greatest thing you can do is to pray for them daily.

I asked several couples who have remarried and have gone through some struggles with teenage stepchildren to share what they did to resolve the problems they faced. Their answers are interesting and helpful. From each conversation, we can gain an insight.

"The talks"

Until we sat down and talked intelligently and objectively about our problems, we never seemed to make progress. Our stepson was belligerent, but desperately wanting to see things change. So did we. As we look back on those hard times, it was the "talks" we had that did it. He respected us for wanting to talk things out, and slowly but surely he began to respond to us as his parents. Today he relates to us in a wonderful way, calling us "Mother" and "Dad" without any hesitation.

Insight: The importance of talking things out with your teenage stepchild.

"My new wife is number one"

Our son gave us a great deal of trouble after I remarried. He wanted to live with me rather than his mother since she had left us for another man. When I finally remarried, he refused to relate to my new wife as his mother. He ignored her, rebelled at her wishes, and almost broke up our marriage. The change came the day I sat down with him and told him that my new wife was number one now in my life, and that she came before he did in my list of priorities. He was shocked at what I said, and it took him several weeks to see that it was true. Finally, he said to my wife one day, "Well, it looks like my dad really likes you and is going to keep you around for good, so I guess I'd better learn to live with it. I'm sorry for the way I have acted. I'll try to do better." She grabbed him and gave him a big hug and kiss, and things have been much better ever since.

Insight: Establish the priority of your marital partner in front of your teenage stepchild.

"With God's help, I could love that girl"

My husband and I had problems from the start. He made the decision to keep his teenage daughter without asking me my opinion or approval. I inherited his daughter under difficult circumstances. She hated me and was constantly doing things to hurt me. When my husband would come home she would turn on the sweetness for him. He would always take her side when she and I had a disagreement. Frankly, my response to him went down to almost zero! I was becoming quite bitter toward him as well as her. I went for counseling, hoping to get some sympathy for my situation. What I was told was both good and bad. I learned that I had made a mistake in not confronting my husband about this matter before we were married. I also learned that I had to deal with this problem no matter whose fault it was to start with. That hurt. I was hoping someone would tell me it was OK to get rid of that girl. I learned that I had to respond to her as though she were my own child, and that with God's help and power, I could love anyone on earth, including my teenage stepdaughter. That hurt all the more. The real problem I discovered was that God was showing me my lack of His love by giving me a situation that really tested my love. I soon realized that I had failed the test. No need to get upset and bitter over it. I had to face it. In my own strength I couldn't handle it. But with God's help, I could love that girl as much as I could love my own daughter. Praise the Lord, it happened! It started to change the moment I confessed my wrong attitudes and rebellion toward my husband and my teenaged stepdaughter. I began to pray more, and to ask God to help me love that girl. He answered that prayer, and today, many years later, she is very special to me, and I love her as though she were my own daughter. We are very close.

Insight: Seek God's help for your relationship with your teenage stepchildren, especially His wonderful love.

"We were like two families trying to be one"

Our problems centered in matters of responsibility and acceptance. We had two children, one belonged to me, and the other to my husband. It seemed natural to respond to your own child in a more accepting way than to your stepchild. We both had difficulty with this. One of the first problems dealt with allowances. My husband gave more money to his son than he did to my daughter, even though my daughter was older than his son. None of his explanations were satisfactory. Further problems arose at Christmas and birthdays. I spent more money on my daughter than on his son, and my husband did the same toward his boy. We were like two families trying to be one. His son never felt that I accepted him, and my daughter never felt accepted by my husband. When things needed to be done in the way of jobs around the home, I asked more of his son than I did my daughter, and my husband did the same. This had to stop. Finally, my husband decided to get some professional help. His counselor encouraged him to do all things equally, and to discuss this with everyone at a family meeting. He was told by the counselor that an open admission of the problem would help bring a solution. So, my husband called a family meeting. He asked us all to give him two hours one night without interruptions. I was so proud of him that night. He admitted that he favored his son, and he apologized to my daughter. Of course, I did the same. It was easier than I thought it would be. The next thing he did was divide up the responsibilities around the house so everyone had an equal share of the work load. We had a few arguments over that, but a final solution was worked out to everyone's satisfaction. The biggest change came when he shared about money. He decided to give the children an equal amount of the family income each month with which they must learn to buy all of their clothes and pay for all of their entertainment and extra meals and snacks, etc. He got them each a checkbook and helped them set up a budget and then put them on their own. The change of atmosphere in our home has been amazing. Both of them now feel accepted and responsible. Another little thing really helped. He said that at mealtimes we would all hold hands together while we prayed and thanked the Lord for our food, and that each person would pray, rotating each meal.

Insight: Treat your stepchildren on an equal basis with your own children.

Much more could be said about the problems of teenage stepchildren. These four couples faced their problems and came up with some solutions that worked for them. They may not work for you in exactly the same way, but the insights make sense. Let's review them.

1. Learn to talk things over with your teenage stepchildren.
2. Establish the priority of your marital partner in front of your teenage stepchildren.
3. Seek God's help for your relationship with your teenage stepchildren, especially His wonderful love.
4. Treat your stepchildren on an equal basis with your own children.

Problem No. 3—How Do You Treat the Former Partner?

The third practical problem which remarried couples must face with respect to their stepchildren is the treatment of former partners. If you think there will be no problem along this line, guess again. Every remarried couple that I interviewed who had stepchildren spoke about this problem. Each case is different, of course, and the way the former partner is treated depends much upon the circumstances that caused the divorce.

Visiting rights vary greatly from couple to couple. Some want to see their children and can't, and others don't want to see their children even though they can have that privilege. Here is a partial list of some of the practical problems you must face, as given to me by remarried couples:

1. What you call the former partner when he or she calls or visits.
2. What rules you have for visits by former partners.
3. Should former partners be allowed in your house?
4. How you handle any disagreements over the care of the children.
5. What to do when one of your stepchildren wants to go live with a former partner.
6. How to handle the gifts a former partner brings to your stepchildren.
7. What privileges you give to the relatives of your former partner who still relate to your stepchildren as part of their family.
8. How to deal with frequent telephone calls by the former partner wanting to talk with your stepchildren.
9. What to say to your stepchild about the motives and actions of a former partner that you believe are wrong.
10. What to tell your child to say to a former partner when the child is asked about his new family relationships.
11. How to handle the holidays and the desires of former partners to be with their children on these special days.
12. What to tell your children about responding to grandparents whom they have inherited, as well as the extended family of the stepparent.

This list could go on and on. Each family situation has its own peculiar difficulties that must be faced and worked out. Rather than try to deal with each particular, I have tried to list some general principles that will affect all kinds of situations.

General Principles in Relating to Former Partners

1. *Never criticize or downgrade a former partner in front of the child.*

You may desire to do so, but avoid the temptation like a plague! It will not help your relationship to a stepchild if you constantly criticize that child's real parent.

Mary Ingerson was insecure in her relationship to her husband, Fred. His former wife was very attractive, and although she had left Fred for another man, she constantly made her presence felt in Mary's life through her daughter. Mary had great difficulties relating to her stepdaughter because of the girl's feelings toward her real mother. When the stepdaughter would say something good about her mother, Mary felt obliged to bring out some negative point. Mary tried to downgrade her stepdaughter's real mother whenever she could, thinking that this would help her stepchild learn the "real truth" about her mother. It didn't work. The stepchild became bitter toward her stepmother, and, of course, more and more defensive and supportive of her real mother. Mary's pride was getting in the way, and until she faced up to this problem, things would get worse.

Fred helped a great deal one day when he told Mary that she was ten thousand times a better wife than his former wife. He told her to stop comparing herself with his former wife, and above all, to stop all the negative remarks. It was hindering his own response to her. Mary got the point real fast. She apologized to Fred and her stepchild, and asked them to pray for her so that she could stop the critical remarks. Things really changed after that. Her stepchild started to relate to her as she would to her own mother and Mary became a much happier and more secure person.

2. *Request that the former partner always deal with his or her former mate, not with the new partner.*

Jean, a lady friend of ours, has a very difficult time talking with her husband's former wife. This woman gives Jean her opinions about how to raise her children whom she left with her husband years ago. It is hard for Jean, the new wife, to be sweet and kind when she sees this former partner deliberately causing trouble. I called Jean's husband and told him about the situation, and he said, "Well, my wife has to learn how to deal with my former wife!" I said, "No she doesn't. You should tell your former wife that if she has any suggestions to make or problems to resolve, she is to talk with you only, not with Jean." He seemed surprised to hear me say that to him for he hadn't realized that it was such a problem to Jean. I urged him to protect Jean from his former wife's attempts to upset her and make her feel incompetent in handling the children. He responded well, and the interesting thing that happened is that his former wife stopped her constant calling.

3. *Do not resent the gifts that your former partner brings to the children.*

Yes, this is a difficult problem. But, you do not help matters by resenting the gifts that the former partner brings or gives to the children. Your children will learn the difference between mere gifts and real love. Also, remember that the former partner still loves the child, and wants desperately to communicate that love by means of gifts. The child will soon realize whether it is genuine or not. When you try to destroy the value of those gifts in your children's minds, you do much harm to your relationship with those stepchildren.

John Carrington was really upset with the lavish gifts which his wife's former husband would bring to his stepson. He did not handle it very well and he felt threatened because he could not afford such gifts. He talked with me one day about it, and I encouraged him not to attack the value of those gifts in front of his stepson, but to explain how happy he was for his stepson to receive those gifts which he himself could not afford. I told him to be honest and open with his stepson about his ability to afford such "nice things," and to reassure his stepson of his love by spending time with him, even enjoying the gifts which the boy's real father had given to him. John accepted what I had to say, and immediately knew what he should do. The boy's real father had purchased a very expensive train set for his son that John could not afford. John had refused to play with his son when he wanted to play with the train set. John went right home that day after work and had a marvelous time playing with his stepson and that train set.

4. *Be very clear with your former partner about the details involved when a visit with the children occurs.*

When the former partner has the legal right to visit the children, this always presents some tense moments and makes for difficult relationships. Often these brief moments between the former partners are times of criticism and anger; arguments about the children are not infrequent. The children are caught between the parents and stepparents and end up being confused and resentful.

Do not allow a former partner to promise to the child that he or she will pick him up at a certain time, and then show up three hours later, or worse yet, not at all. Make it clear that you expect promises to be kept. Do not tolerate a former partner's negligence in this regard. You do not have to do that. If that partner wants visiting privileges, then he or she must conform to the details of those arrangements.

Also, do not allow your former partner to keep changing dates and times, and asking for special privileges not in the original agreements. This develops insecurity in the children, and usually results in great pressure and inconvenience to you. Many former partners use these tactics to hurt their former partners. They know what they are doing, and you must not allow it.

5. *Always refer to the former partner as "your dad" or "your mother" in front of the stepchild.*

In spite of your desires to be known as "Dad" or "Mother" to your stepchild, don't undermine the child's understanding or confidence by not calling the real father and mother of the child as the child would do. To say to your stepchild, "Sheila's on the phone and wants to talk to you," instead of, "Your mother wants to talk to you," will only deepen your stepchild's resentment of you.

6. *Don't force your stepchild to choose sides.*

It's hard enough for the stepchild to adjust to a new parent. Don't force the child to choose between the former parent and the stepparent. Your remarriage has brought with it certain adjustments that must be made. One adjustment for your child is to accept his real parent and his stepparent with equal respect and love. That's not easy for anyone, let alone a little child.

Dan Murcer was very unhappy about his stepson's love for his real father. He told his stepson one day, "Make up your mind who you want for your father. It's him or me. You can't have both!" Dan made a big mistake. A stepchild must learn to respond to both, and Dan was making it difficult. It's not an "either/or" situation; it's a "both/and" problem! Help your child respond to both kinds of parents. Don't make him choose sides. The child will have a difficult time handling that kind of divided loyalty. It is much better to encourage the child to relate to both parents as though they were his own. The child has the capacity to love them both and respect them both.

7. *Teach your child to show respect and love for the extended family.*

This will be a very important lesson for your child's future relationships with other people. Don't hinder the child from treating his stepfamily with love as he would his own family. In fact, you should encourage it. Allow the grandparents of the former partner to relate to the children as they have always done. Also, give the grandparents of the new partner the same privilege.

People have great capacities for love. We do not help the children by making them hesitant in responding to others, whether in a stepfamily situation or in the church or in society in general.

I have observed that grandparents can be a special blessing to children of broken homes and in remarriage situations. They have the ability to relate to the children without the pressure that the child's parents feel. A step-grandparent can be just the right person to help a stepchild overcome the adjustment problems he will experience in his new environment.

We have discussed just three basic practical problems which remarried families experience in dealing with children who are not their own. Of course, many more could be added to this list. We have tried to be practical and careful to relate to all kinds of situations. We may not have succeeded in your case. But, don't give up—God has a solution, and His power can change that difficult situation you now face. It is a difficult assignment to raise children who are not your own, but it can be so rewarding. One day you will be thankful for all the tears, heartaches, hassles, and arguments. God will reward your faithfulness to Him and to those children He has placed under your care. Even though they were not your own originally, you can make them your own emotionally and mentally. May God give you His patience and strength for your difficult assignment.

Questions for Reflection

1. How can problems dealing with child custody be resolved without going to court?
2. What have you done to make your stepchild feel fully accepted and loved by you?
3. Why do you think stepparents seem to be lenient toward their stepchildren when it comes to discipline?

4. What insights were shared by remarried couples who have raised teenage stepchildren?
5. What kinds of problems do you face in reference to your stepchild's relationship to his real parents?
6. What should you do about any problems that a former partner is causing in your relationship to your stepchildren?
7. How should you handle a child's devotion to his or her real parent?

9

Never Give Up!

"I can't take it anymore!" These words from a Christian wife who had been remarried for several years expressed the hopeless situation in which she found herself every day. Her expectations were high when she married for the third time. The man was a Christian, and seemed to be strong spiritually. He had a good job and an excellent salary. Their marriage brought together her child and his child, and it looked like this new family was going to be blessed of God.

The trouble started when she couldn't measure up to his expectations. He became quite judgmental of his wife and family. Without realizing it, he put much pressure upon them to meet his standards. His first wife was unfaithful to him, and it almost seemed as if he were trying to prevent that from happening again, when in reality he was driving his present wife away from him.

The accusations, suspicions, and arguments continued to increase until the pressure in their marriage and family was unbelievable. The wife could not take it anymore. She tried often to find relief, prayed much about it, and went many times for counseling.

The problem in that marriage? A lack of God's love! The children and the wife were not accepted as they were. Instead, they were expected to perform and to change. The self-image of that wife was reduced to almost nothing, and the children were also affected. The husband needed to be broken in spirit, and filled with the forgiving love of God for his family. His pride was keeping him from experiencing the love and affection which his family wanted to give him.

Is this situation hopeless? Is there no answer but to break up another marriage and another family? We may quickly respond that no marriage is beyond hope. We know that God is able to put things back together again. Christians know that and believe that, but what do you do when the situation seems hopeless and the pressure upon you is so intense?

Praise the Lord that this marriage was restored after the husband was confronted by a Christian friend. At first it was hard for him to admit his lack of love, but when he did, a great burden was lifted. The first thing he did that gradually changed his life was to memorize 1 Corinthians 13. He asked God to help him respond according to the qualities of love which he saw in that biblical passage.

I'm thankful for many remarried couples who manifest love, joy, and maturity in their marriages. It's a great encouragement to see people begin again and make it successfully. Praise the Lord! But, I would be less than honest if I did not tell you that many remarriages are unhappy. People make mistakes and often marry someone too quickly. It's difficult to break years of habit with one person and try to live in the same house with someone with an entirely different personality and temperament.

Tom and Jennifer were excited about getting married. Both of them had lost their first partners to other people. This marriage seemed right for both of them. They were willing to work at making it all that God wanted it to be. The ceremony was simple, but beautiful. After a short honeymoon, they settled in their new home, and tried to handle the four children that Jennifer had by her previous marriage. Within a few weeks, it was obvious that they were headed for trouble. Tom hated little kids, and Jennifer's kids were driving him crazy. He constantly criticized Jennifer for not taking care of them. He showed no affection for the children, and his love for Jennifer was noticeably weakened. Jennifer would cry a great deal and plead with him to understand her difficulties with raising four children. She thought that he was going to help her in that task, but instead, he added to her burdens. It became so unbearable that Jennifer was losing control of her emotions almost every day. She could no longer stand the sight of Tom. She began to hate him for his attitudes toward her children, and ultimately, toward herself. Tom became interested in a girl at his office. He started staying late and coming home around 9:00 P.M. One day, he didn't come home. Jennifer knew he was with that girl, and her resentment and hatred was so great that she thought she would have a nervous breakdown. When he came home two days later and made a bunch of excuses, she blew up at him, and told him to get out of the house and never come back again.

Is this marriage hopeless? Can nothing be done to straighten things out? Where is God at a time like this? The questions filled Jennifer's mind, and the answers were not coming very easily.

I had the difficult task of confronting Tom about his attitudes and his affair with the girl in his office. Tom was very defensive at first, but slowly he changed his attitude when he realized that I sincerely loved him. We started to meet regularly. He began to open his heart to me, and started to respond to God's Word like he had never done before. Within a few months, he and Jennifer were not only coping with the situation but were actually enjoying each other and the children.

While I was busy in my office one day preparing a message, my secretary interrupted with an urgent call from a lady who was desperate. Her husband had beaten her up for the third time and she didn't know what to do. When she married him, she thought that he would be sweet and kind to her. Her first husband was an alcoholic and eventually left her because he couldn't stand her commitment to Jesus Christ. He hated the Bible, her church, and everything that she ever said about her faith. After several years alone, she decided to remarry. Her husband was so romantic and sweet to her during the days of her courtship, she never dreamed that he would be violent and physically strike her. When it happened the first time, she excused it and since he asked for forgiveness and said he was really sorry, she accepted his words and forgot it. About two years later, he hit her again, only this time he couldn't stop. He left her with many bruises on her body, and she stayed in the house for about ten weeks, telling her friends that she was sick. Now, six months later, he had done it again, and she was desperate, not knowing what to do, or how to respond to him.

The first thing I told her to do was to leave the house and go stay with a friend. Then I called her husband and made an appointment with him. He was reluctant until I told him that I knew what he had done, and that his wife would not be there when he got home from his office that day. After work he came to see me. He was very defensive and tried to justify his actions. He left the office mad, and demanded that I tell him where his wife was. I refused. The next thing I did was to have one of our city police officers and one of our church elders see him about this. He was in serious trouble, but he had not realized it until the two men showed up at his door. Immediately he knew that he needed help. He started a series of counseling sessions with a Christian psychologist. This helped deliver him from his hostility within a year's time, and today he and his wife are happily married and living without fear.

Pastors and marriage counselors hear about such situations all of the time. People get desperate and don't know where to turn or what to do. Are all these cases hopeless? We know that many do end up in divorce, but do they have to end that way? What alternatives do people have who find themselves in a "hopeless situation"? Before we answer that, let's evaluate the kinds of situations that people say are hopeless. What are the common characteristics? Maybe some of these things are happening to you right now. Perhaps we can help you to understand your situation and be prepared for what you may have to face in the future.

Common Characteristics of Hopeless Situations

1. *They always appear to be greater than what we can handle by ourselves.*

You can always tell when a marriage is facing serious problems and things are reaching the point of no return. The conflicts appear to be so great that the individuals involved are not capable of coping with or correcting them.

The wife or the husband may say, "I can't take it anymore!" "Things have gone too far!" "He (or she) will never change!" When either marriage partner starts talking like this, the marriage is on the verge of being destroyed. It appears hopeless indeed.

2. *The fear and anxiety in our hearts seem to be greater than we can bear.*

Remarried people begin with insecurity. This often grows in a remarriage, rather than going away. Much depends upon the maturity and love of the partners. The first fear is usually that of self-esteem. We begin to lose confidence in ourselves, fearing that we may somehow be responsible for the hopeless situation that is now developing. The fear of rejection, of course, will often come when our marital partner is not responding to us as we need and desire. The fear of loss and failure will also capture our hearts in such times. If a previous marriage failed, what will people think if this one fails? What does that say about my ability to make someone happy?

I have seen remarried people so nervous and fearful that they physically shake. I have seen many tears and heartaches among the remarried. My heart goes out to these people when I know they are facing situations that to them seem hopeless and beyond recovery.

3. *They cause us to question God and His promises.*

A frequent statement is "Why, Pastor, is God doing this to me?" Others will say it this way, "Why is God allowing this to happen?" Or some say, "What have I done to make God do this to me?" These questions are often raised by someone who faces a hopeless situation and has no adequate explanation for it. It is frequently asked by Christians who believe that God has a purpose in everything. Their ability to cope with a hopeless situation is often based on their belief that God has a reason for what is happening to them.

4. *The marriage seems to be the major obstacle to personal happiness.*

When people start thinking like this, it usually is not long before the marriage breaks up. When you see your marital situation as the main barrier to your own personal happiness, your marriage will not last unless you do something to change your viewpoint.

Instead of seeing marriage as a blessing, people in a hopeless situation see it as the problem and the obstacle. They begin to believe that they would be much happier if they could get out of the marriage rather than stay with it.

One Christian wife felt that way for some time, and in a conversation with a neighbor one day she was led to believe that divorce would be the answer. She got a divorce in spite of the advice of Christian friends, and today she is extremely unhappy. She listened to the advice of an unbelieving neighbor instead of her Christian friends. You might ask, "How could she do that so easily?" The answer is found in the fact that she had been thinking that way for some time. It was already in her mind. It was relatively easy to do it after this unbelieving neighbor encouraged it. To her, the marriage was a hopeless situation and she viewed it as the major obstacle to her own personal happiness. But she found out that the problem was not her marriage, but herself.

What Causes a Person to Lose Hope and Become Depressed?

Many people are depressed with their marriages. They don't know what to do about it. Things seem so hopeless. They doubt if anything will ever change. What causes a person to get so depressed and to give up hope that the marriage can ever be different?

Every person's situation is a little different from another, and we don't want to oversimplify the serious subject of depression. There are often physical causes behind depression which a medical doctor can help. Sometimes the problem is deeply rooted in your childhood or your temperament. Without ignoring those facts, we want to give a brief analysis of why many remarried people become depressed with their marriage situation.

1. *Unresolved conflicts of the past.*

The depression leaves when the problems are resolved. This is a very common cause of people losing hope. A problem in the past has not been handled properly, and it causes a person to become depressed with the present situation.

2. *Unfulfilled goals or expectations.*

This is seen quite often among the remarried. Past marital failures have increased your expectations. Depression can set in when these expectations are not fulfilled. You can also become very discouraged over the expectations of your partner. When you can't measure up, it becomes an impossible situation.

3. *Unexpected circumstances beyond your control.*

There's nothing you can do about this but live with it. You did not cause it; it simply happened. It might deal with health, finances, children, or occupation. It can lead to serious depression. You begin to think that you made the wrong decision when you decided to remarry.

4. *Unreasonable demands by your partner or your children.*

In some respects, this can lead to depression faster than many of the other points mentioned. We all face these kinds of demands at one time or another. But when the demands are constantly placed upon you, and you either can't or are unwilling to meet them, it causes you to be depressed and to lose hope.

5. *Unfaithful actions by those you trust.*

If your marital partner is unfaithful to you, you may find it difficult to get over emotionally. You think about it often and you have a tendency to give up. If you can't trust your husband or your wife, whom can you trust? Much of the depression I see among remarried couples is definitely related to their inability to trust their partners. Such unfaithful actions may have started in a previous marriage, but they have a tendency to carry over into another marriage. If either marriage partner has experienced the unfaithfulness of a partner before, he or she is more susceptible to the fear of its reoccurrence.

6. *Unconcerned attitudes toward your personal needs and desires.*

Whether an attitude of unconcern is exhibited by your spouse or your children, it still hurts. If it continues, you begin to lose hope, and depression sets in. All of us need love, appreciation, approval, and acceptance. When these are not given, we grow discouraged, depressed, and often become bitter and resentful. We feel that we don't deserve the treatment we are getting.

7. *Unworthy feelings about your relationship to God.*

As a pastor, I see this problem quite a bit among Christians. There is a certain pressure put upon all of us to be what God wants us to be. We are told to study the Bible, pray, give, witness, teach Sunday School, sing in the choir, visit the sick, invite people over to our house for dinner, attend scores of meetings, and to be ready to go to the mission field at any time God calls for us to go!

Remarried people feel the pressure to live up to what the Bible teaches about marriage and the family. If your previous marriage did not work out, you already have one strike against you. It gets worse when you expect your new marriage to be all that an ideal marriage should be. If it doesn't work out that way, you begin feeling that you are not worthy because of what you have done or been in the past. You view yourself as a "sub-Christian," not really a part of the "Spirit-filled" group of Christians who smile most of the time and seem to have great marriages and super families.

Your depression becomes more serious as time goes by and nothing "super spiritual" ever seems to happen to you. You get to thinking that this is the way it is going to be in your life because you got divorced and remarried. It's God's way of dealing with your past mistakes, you think. So, you remain defeated most of the time, and you have definitely given up hope that your marriage will ever change.

What Should You Do in a Hopeless Situation?

Enough of the problems! Let's talk about the solutions.

No matter how desperate you are or how hopeless your marriage seems, do not allow yourself to believe that nothing can change. It can change because of who God is. Never doubt His power to change your situation. He is the God of hope and help.

Also, never interpret your circumstances as evidence that God doesn't love you or care about you. That simply is not true. Even when you do wrong, He loves you. If He cares about a sparrow that falls from the tree, then He cares about you (read Matthew 6:25–34).

When people share the hopelessness of their situation, I get excited, because I believe our hopelessness provides God with a great opportunity to demonstrate His power. I often think of the children of Israel at the Red Sea when the armies of Pharaoh were pursuing them. Now, that's what I call a hopeless situation! In Exodus 14:11, 12 we read of their frightened response to Moses:

> Is it because there were no graves in Egypt that you have taken us away to die in the wilderness? Why have you dealt with us in this way, bringing us out of Egypt? Is this not the word that we spoke to you in Egypt, saying, "Leave us alone that we may serve the Egyptians"? For it would have been better for us to serve the Egyptians than to die in the wilderness.

As you know, this hopeless situation gave God the opportunity to demonstrate His mighty power. In that same chapter, in verses 30 and 31, we read this summary:

> Thus the Lord saved Israel that day from the hand of the Egyptians, and Israel saw the Egyptians dead on the seashore. And when Israel

saw the great power which the Lord had used against the Egyptians, the people feared the Lord, and they believed in the Lord and in His servant Moses.

God has great power to change our circumstances. The above situation was used by God to cause His people to believe in Him. That might very well happen in your case also. God may have given you a tough assignment in a bad marriage because He wants to use it to bring people to faith in Him. He might do it through changing your situation when everyone says it cannot be changed. Your bad marriage may become a blessed and happy one by the power of God and everyone will know that God did it.

When people ask what they should do when they find themselves in a difficult marriage and in what seems to be a hopeless situation, I offer the following four things:

1. *Put your faith in God's plan and control of all things.*

Joseph's brothers sold him into slavery to Egypt. In Genesis 50:18–21, the brothers were confronted with Joseph as the mighty ruler of Egypt, next to Pharaoh himself. They fell down before him and said, "We are your servants." Joseph told them not to be afraid but to realize the overall plan of God. He said, "And as for you, you meant evil against me, but God meant it for good in order to bring about this present result, to preserve many people alive."

God is causing all things to work together for our good and His glory, even when it doesn't look like it from our point of view.

2. *Understand that God has a specific purpose for your situation.*

Ultimately, all things were created and are allowed to exist by God so that He will be glorified by what takes place. To glorify God ought to be our highest purpose in life. We must understand that God has a special purpose in everything.

When Paul was in prison in Rome, it looked like a hopeless situation. Believers were afraid for his life, wondering why God would allow this to happen. Yet, Paul had one of his greatest opportunities to share the gospel while he was a prisoner. He wrote in Philippians 1:12–14:

> Now I want you to know, brethren, that my circumstances have turned out for the greater progress of the gospel, so that my imprisonment in the cause of Christ has become well known throughout the whole praetorian guard and to everyone else, and that most of the brethren, trusting in the Lord because of my imprisonment, have far more courage to speak the word of God without fear.

3. *Depend upon God and what He can do, and relax!*

Much of our anxiety is related to our lack of dependence upon God. Our trust is in our own ability to cope with the bad situation, or in the help of others to change it, rather than in the One whom we should trust, God Himself. He loves us, and He wants us to depend upon Him. Philippians 4:13 says, "I can do all things through Him who strengthens me." Ephesians 3:20 says He is "able to do exceeding abundantly beyond all that we ask or think, according to the power that works within us."

4. *Give praise and thanks to God for all that He is and has done and is going to do in your situation.*

First Thessalonians 5:18 says, "in everything give thanks; for this is God's will for you in Christ Jesus." Are you able to thank God for your marital situation? No matter how hopeless it seems, you will not be able to endure it without a thankful heart. That seems strange to us—thanking God for a hopeless situation. It's hard to do. You feel so insincere. But, even though you don't inwardly feel like doing it, do it anyway. On the basis of your knowledge of God and His ways, you can thank Him for what He is going to do through all of it.

Philippians 4:6, 7 teaches us that the peace we are looking for in our troubled lives and marriages comes through prayer "with thanksgiving." The opposite is to worry and be filled with anxiety. Bring your burdens and requests to God, and thank Him for what He is going to do through your difficult situation that to you, seems very hopeless. It's not hopeless to God. He knows what He intends to do with it, and with you. Trust Him. He really loves you!

Questions for Reflection

1. What are the common characteristics of a hopeless situation?
2. Have you been through such a situation in your life? What brought you out of it?
3. Are you going through such a situation now? What steps can you take to cope with it?
4. What causes a person to lose hope and get depressed?
5. What should you do if you find yourself in a situation that appears hopeless?

10

Remember Your Vows

After hours of interviews and evaluations with many remarried people, I found myself asking this question: "What is their greatest need?" It is one thing to analyze the experiences of people and to write about their problems; it is quite another thing to deal with their greatest need.

One husband told me in answer to my question: "I'm not sure I know. We've got many needs and we're struggling to make our marriage something that our previous marriages never were. My biggest problem is learning how to love my wife the way God wants me to do. I need help in this area. I know it's not enough to say 'I love you.' That's important. But, there has to be more than words. I need to love my wife in the middle of our problems—when things aren't going too good."

One wife answered my question this way: "My greatest need is to be loved by my present husband like my former husband never did!"

Another wife, who was obviously under a great deal of

pressure, responded: "My greatest need is to get away from that man! He's driving me crazy! I can't stand his constant judgments!" Another wife said, "My greatest need is to have my husband love my children. I know it's hard for him to love kids who are not his own, but if he doesn't start doing it soon, I don't see much hope for our situation." Another wife said, "I've got many needs, but if my husband really loved me, I think a lot of them would go away."

Behind all these answers which demonstrate the great need of love, is the matter of commitment. Remarried people remember the words of former partners who said, "I love you"; but the words lost their meaning and value through the divorce that broke up the marriage. The real concern now is that of commitment. Will the love endure? Will my present partner's assurances of love and loyalty be more than what my former partner displayed?

Consider what Solomon said about the importance of commitment and love in Song of Solomon 8:6, 7:

Put me like a seal over your heart, like a seal on your arm. For love is as strong as death, jealousy is as severe as Sheol (the grave): Its flashes are flashes of fire, the very flame of the Lord. Many waters cannot quench love, nor will rivers overflow it; If a man were to give all the riches of his house for love, it would be utterly despised.

If there is one great fear in the heart of a remarried person, it is that the marriage will not last. Joan Andrews said in her interview: "I keep wondering whether this marriage will make it or not. Will my husband now be more faithful than my first husband? I don't want to be suspicious, but I can't help it. I pray every day that this one will last."

Rebecca Brown said somewhat the same thing during the interview I had with her and her husband, Steve. She loves Steve, but she fears at times that he will not come home one day. Her first husband ran off with another woman. She said, "I hate myself for not trusting Steve. When he comes home late from the office, I can hardly stand it. I keep worrying about his loyalty to me." I told Steve that he should always call his wife whenever he must be late, and reassure her of his love and loyalty. I also told him not to make it a habit of coming home late. It would have a tendency to produce more anxiety in his wife's heart.

Jesus said, "What therefore God has joined together, let no man separate." Strong words! Whatever broke up your previous marriage, don't let anything or anyone do it again. Determine to be faithful to your partner no matter what. Sure there are problems and pressures to face, but none of those difficulties should be allowed to undermine your commitment to your marital partner.

Renew Your Vows

Have you thought about your vows lately? Do you remember what you said? If they were not all that strong, why not have a "Renewal of Vows Ceremony"? Your kids can participate and they will love it! You could plan it on your wedding anniversary. You might have your pastor participate, or Christian friends who are close to you. This outside participation increases the circle of accountability.

The following brief outline can give you some idea of what can be done.

1. Play some wedding music or have someone sing songs about commitment.
2. Read Scripture—such as Ephesians 5:22–33 and 1 John 4:7–21.

3. Ask a pastor or another friend to comment on the Scripture, or rehearse the facts about your past and your desire to make your remarriage what God wants it to be.
4. Let the children participate in music, or the reading of Scripture, or to say something about what they want their family to be.
5. Have a pastor or friend ask you the following questions to which you can respond "I do" at the end:

To Husband: "Do you, John, recommit yourself to Mary, before God and these witnesses? Do you once again pledge your loyalty to her and to her alone until death parts you? Do you desire to honor your wife at all times, refusing to criticize her in front of the children or others? Do you promise again to provide for all her needs as well as for the family your marriage has brought together? Do you accept without any hesitation the responsibility of spiritual leadership in your home, and do you promise to lead your family in Bible reading and prayer on a regular basis? Do you realize that your basic responsibility is to love your wife as Jesus Christ loved His church, and do you once again dedicate yourself to the fulfillment of this responsibility?"

(If so, you may answer, "I do.")

To Wife: "Do you, Mary, recommit yourself to John, before God and these witnesses? Do you once again pledge your loyalty to him and to him alone until death parts you? Do you promise again to love and support your husband, seeking to be the help God wants you to be? Do you desire to honor your husband in front of the children and others, refusing to criticize him or reduce his leadership role in their eyes?"

(If so, you may answer, "I do.")

6. Repeat the following vows to each other, after answering the above questions:

Husband: "I, John, recommit myself to you, Mary, before God and these witnesses. I promise once again to be the spiritual leader of our home, and to provide for your needs as well as those of our family. I will honor and respect you at all times. I will refuse to share our intimacies with anyone else without your permission. I once again pledge my loyalty to you alone, forsaking all others, until the Lord comes or death parts us. I love you."

Wife: "I, Mary, recommit myself to you, John, before God and these witnesses. I promise once again to love and support you in your leadership of our home. I will honor and respect you at all times. I will refuse to share our intimacies with anyone else without your permission. I once again pledge my loyalty to you alone, forsaking all others, until the Lord comes or death parts us. I love you."

7. Give a big hug and kiss to each other—then both of you to each of the children.

8. Exchange a small token or gift of remembrance to each other as an additional pledge of your love and loyalty.

Before you ignore what I just said, or think that this suggestion of a "Renewal of Vows Ceremony" is a waste of time, let me challenge you with this thought: What harm could it do? Is it possible that it might really strengthen your present marriage?

I have used this ceremony and ones like it in various marriage seminars in different parts of the country. The response has been outstanding. Many couples have expressed to me how much it meant to them to recommit themselves to each other in such a public ceremony.

One couple from Sacramento, California, wrote: "This renewal of vows was just what we needed. We were both married once before and we still suffer from our divorces. When we looked into each other's eyes (like you said we had to do!) and repeated those vows, we both started crying. It was the best thing we could have done. Thank you so much for asking us to participate. It has changed our relationship to each other these past few weeks."

Another couple from the Northwest said: "We had been really struggling with our marriage when we decided to come to your seminar. Most of what you said we already knew, but we were not living it. What made the difference was when you asked us to repeat those vows to each other. My husband broke down and cried when he came to the part about 'forsaking all others.' He confessed that he had been flirting with one of the girls in his office, and he asked for my forgiveness. Our love for each other has really grown since that moment. Thanks for asking us to do it."

One husband from Southern California wrote: "The toughest thing I've done in a long time was to say those vows to my wife. I really haven't been the husband I should be to her. Her former husband has given me a lot of hassle, and I guess I've let that affect me in the way I treat her. With God's help, things are going to change. Saying those vows to her really shook me up!"

Several years ago I counseled a remarried couple who had many problems and lots of reasons for giving up on their marriage. I challenged them to have a "Renewal of Vows Ceremony" in front of their families and friends. They said, "Can't we do it in private, Pastor, here in your office?" I responded, "It needs to be seen and heard by your family and your friends. It makes you accountable to them, plus it will be used by God to reinforce the marriages of others." They said they would do it, and in about three weeks, they had the ceremony at a local park. The impact was tremendous. One of the couples who attended were not getting along well in their marriage, and they testify today that seeing this "Renewal of Vows Ceremony" got them back together again.

Don't criticize this idea, until you've tried it. I believe that it has the potential of restoring your love for each other as well as strengthening your commitment to your marriage and family. The more of your friends who witness it, the better.

Spiritual Commitment

One reason why some commitments are not sufficient and do not last, is because they lack spiritual depth and meaning. Commitments are strong when they are reinforced by a sense of accountability. The greatest accountability that any of us have is to God Himself.

Spiritual commitment begins with your faith in God and His Word. You sense your accountability to Him and what He says. Hebrews 11:6 says, "And without faith it is impossible to please Him, for he who comes to God must believe that He is, and that He is a rewarder of those who seek Him." Do you believe that there is a God to whom you are personally accountable? Romans 14:12 states, "So then each one of us shall give account of himself to God."

Ecclesiastes 5:4 says, "When you make a vow to God, do not be late in paying it, for He takes no delight in fools. Pay what you vow!" It is a very serious matter before God when you make a vow or promise, and do not keep it. No matter what circumstances come into your marriage or feelings of despair over what seems to be a hopeless situation, your vow still stands. You are accountable to God.

True fear of the Lord prevents you from doing the wrong thing. Proverbs 16:6 says, "By the fear of the Lord one keeps away from evil." The depth of your spiritual commitment is the key for making your marriage work.

Spiritual commitment does not grow in a vacuum. It is nurtured and developed by prayer and continual dependency upon God's Word, the Bible. Proverbs 3:5, 6 puts it this way:

> Trust in the Lord with all your heart, and do not lean on your own understanding. In all your ways acknowledge Him, and He will make your paths straight.

Don't think that your profession of faith in Jesus Christ will guarantee your commitment to your marital partner. Christians experience divorce and the breakup of families as surely as non-Christians. In most cases, the seeds of decay are planted in hearts that do not sense their accountability to God nor daily depend upon God in prayer and obedience to His Word.

A good Bible teacher and leader left his wife and family and ran off with another woman. Many people were shocked. How could he do this? I had the opportunity to deal with this situation and discovered that the man was living dangerously as a Christian because he was not depending upon God in prayer. He rarely prayed except to thank God for his food at mealtimes. Jesus said in Matthew 26:41, "Keep watching and praying, that you may not enter into temptation; the spirit is willing, but the flesh is weak." If we do not pray, how can we avoid falling into temptation? Are we trusting the Lord to sustain us, or do we think we would never fall?

First Corinthians 10:12, 13 reminds us:

> Therefore let him who thinks he stands take heed lest he fall. No temptation has overtaken you but such as is common to man; and

God is faithful, who will not allow you to be tempted beyond what you are able, but with the temptation will provide the way of escape also, that you may be able to endure it.

Spiritual commitment means you are dependent upon God's grace and power and you do not trust yourself to be strong in a crisis; rather you trust the Lord alone.

I took a survey once in a church among married couples regarding various matters, including spiritual commitment. This church is a Bible-teaching church and the people seem active in evangelism and ministry to one another. One of the questions was: "Do you have a special time of private prayer each day?" Out of one hundred twelve people who filled out the survey (all of whom professed to be Christians), only thirty-two of them answered in the affirmative. A second question was: "Do you read the Bible each day for your own spiritual development?" Only nine people said that they did on a regular basis. Twelve others read the Bible on certain occasions, twenty said they read it at least once a week, and seventy-one said they did not read the Bible at all!

If this survey is representative of the spiritual commitment of Christians, it is no wonder that so many marital problems are occurring in Christian homes. We need God's help—desperately! Without Him, we are open to all kinds of temptation and attack that can destroy our families.

The great need among remarried couples is spiritual commitment. That commitment is to God first, and then to your marital partner, and to your children. God's love is based on a strong commitment. There are no conditional statements like, "I'll continue to love you *if . . .*" or "I'll be loyal *until. . . .*"

Remember your vows!

REMEMBER YOUR VOWS!

REMEMBER YOUR VOWS!

Questions for Reflection

1. What do remarried couples say is their greatest need? What is yours?
2. What is the great fear in the heart of the remarried person?
3. Have you considered a "Renewal of Vows Ceremony"? Why not write out a proposed ceremony of your own?
4. What do we mean by "spiritual commitment"?
5. Why is spiritual commitment so necessary for your remarriage?

A Confidential Questionnaire

This "Confidential Questionnaire" was prepared by two pastor friends, Paul Hoffman and Michael Moore. They specialize in premarital and marital counseling, dealing often with the problems of divorce and remarriage. In addition to basic information that is requested, the following fifteen questions are asked of each person seeking to be remarried:

1. Where and when were you last married?
2. When were you last divorced?
3. Have you been divorced before, and if so, how many times?
4. Has your former spouse been divorced before, and if so, how many times?
5. Are you a Christian? If so, explain *when* and *how* you became a Christian.
6. Is your former spouse a Christian? If so, please explain *when* and *how* your former spouse became a Christian.

7. Were you given premarital counseling before you were married? If so, please describe what it was like.

8. *Where* and *how often* did you attend church together?

9. Did you or your former spouse seek marriage counseling before your divorce? If so, was it Christian counseling, and what was it like?

10. What were the *real* reasons for the divorce? Please be specific and explain them.

11. Were you or your former spouse involved in another affair involving immorality? If so, please explain its effect upon your marriage.

12. Which one of you filed for the divorce, or was it a joint decision?

13. Is your former spouse engaged, living with another "lover," or remarried now? If so, please explain.

14. Would your former spouse accept you back if you returned? Please explain why or why not.

15. Have you or your spouse attempted to restore your marriage? If so, please explain *who* tried and *how*.

After an individual has filled out the questionnaire, the counselor will review the answers of both persons seeking to be married. Often, some important insights are gained during this review. The questionnaire also requires the name, address, and phone number of the former spouse. Though many people do not want to give out that information, it is required if these pastors are going to do the remarrying. They have found that this information allows them to do effective counseling. Otherwise, they are just "going through the motions."

Pastor Hoffman shared with me how important it is to know about the former spouse. He said that he has called and written former spouses all over the United States. Not too long ago, a lady who was engaged to be remarried came in for premarital counseling. Her former husband lived in Missouri though her home was now in California. Pastor Hoffman made contact with the former husband and had the joy of leading him to Jesus Christ. Now, the lady is faced with the choice of remarrying or being reconciled to her former husband. He always encourages a person to try to be reconciled with the former partner. This is always much better than remarrying without a clear conscience in this regard because he or she will carry this over into the next marriage.

Three important steps are encouraged by these pastors after the questionnaire has been evaluated. These points help them determine the individual's rights and responsibilities in remarriage.

(1) The individual is encouraged to confess any sin surrounding the divorce and enjoy God's forgiveness.

(2) The individual is challenged to consider the possibility of reconciliation with the former spouse—consistent with biblical instruction and guidelines.

(3) The counselor requests the privilege of talking with the former spouse, either by phone or by letter.